Understanding Sustainability Economics

Understanding Sustainability Economics

Towards Pluralism in Economics

Peter Söderbaum

publishing for a sustainable future

London • Sterling, VA

First published by Earthscan in the UK and USA in 2008

Copyright © Peter Söderbaum, 2008

ISBN 978-1-84407-626-0 hardback
 978-1-84407-627-7 paperback

Typeset by FiSH Books, Enfield
Printed and bound in the UK by MPG Books Ltd, Bodmin, Cornwall
Cover design by Susanne Harris

For a full list of publications please contact:

Earthscan
Dunstan House
14a St Cross Street
London EC1N 8XA, UK
Tel: +44 (0)20 7841 1930
Fax: +44 (0)20 7242 1474
Email: earthinfo@earthscan.co.uk
Web: **www.earthscan.co.uk**

22883 Quicksilver Drive, Sterling, VA 20166-2012, USA

Earthscan publishes in association with the International Institute for
Environment and Development

A catalogue record for this book is available from the British Library

Library of Congress Cataloging-in-Publication Data

Söderbaum, Peter, 1937–
    Understanding sustainability economics : towards pluralism in economics /
Peter Söderbaum.
        p. cm.
    Includes bibliographical references and index.
    ISBN 978-1-84407-626-0 (hbk.) — ISBN 978-1-84407-627-7 (pbk.) 1.
Environmental economics. 2. Sustainable development. 3. Economic develop-
ment—Environmental aspects. I. Title.
    HC79.E5S6255 2008
    338.9'27—dc22

                                                                2008015770

The paper used for this book is FSC-certified.
FSC (the Forest Stewardship Council) is an
international network to promote responsible
management of the world's forests.

Mixed Sources
Product group from well-managed
forests and other controlled sources
www.fsc.org Cert no. SGS-COC-2482
© 1996 Forest Stewardship Council

Contents

List of Figures and Tables

Figures

Tables

Preface

In various parts of the world, referencing economics as a discipline has increasingly become equal to referencing neoclassical economics. A specific paradigm (theoretical perspective) dominates the scene and many have accepted this simplistic idea of economics as the only possibility. An army of professors at departments of economics have echoed the view that there is only one kind of economics and they have been successful in affecting the mental maps of university students, politicians, business leaders and other actors in society. The institutional framework of our society, from the local to the global, has largely been designed with reference to the principles of neoclassical economics. International institutions, such as the World Trade Organization, the World Bank and the International Monetary Fund, are the products of this specific type of economics and something similar can be said about the European Union with its 'inner market' and connected ideas about competition and progress in society.

In some sense nothing is wrong with the repeated reference to neoclassical economics. This is the dominant paradigm or theoretical perspective and it is still playing an important role. The fact that a large number of actors have internalized the conceptual framework and ideology of neoclassical economics suggests that this theory is somewhat useful to understanding present economies and how they can be managed. But it should always be remembered that this conceptual framework is specific in ideological terms. Neoclassical economics is not neutral in terms of values and ideology. It reduces human beings to consumers, wage earners and investors and does not deal with our role as citizens and professionals in a democratic society. It reduces organizations to business companies and assumes that the role of business is exclusively to focus on monetary profits. It suggests simplistic ideas of progress in society, about efficiency in the economy, about international trade and so on.

This ideological specificity, or 'bias' if you like, has become more of a problem in recent years. Why should economics as a science be limited to one particular ideology at the expense of other points of view? Neoclassical economists often refer to the 'opportunity cost principle' as the hallmark of their discipline, implying that one should always think in terms of choice and alternatives. But they never apply this principle to the level of paradigms. As a specific interest group (understandable in terms of their own 'public choice theory'), they seldom mention competing theoretical perspectives or paradigms, or, at best, refer to alternative perspectives that have little relevance in our present world.

But meaningful and useful alternatives to the mainstream of economics have always existed and today are perhaps more relevant than previously. Students of economics have been protesting about the 'autistic' way of teaching economics at our universities; broad social movements, locally and internationally, regard neoclassical economics as an important part of the problems rather than any solution, and neoclassical economics does not go well with the recent debate about unsustainable trends with respect to health, poverty, social security and the environment. A pluralistic attitude is called for where the opportunity cost principle is applied also at the level of paradigms in economics. Some of the alternatives to neoclassical theory have a lot to offer as part of this debate.

The history of economic ideas tells us a story that does not support the present monopoly claims of neoclassical economists. In the present book, a version of institutional economics is emphasized but this is just one approach among many possibilities. I believe, however, that articulating one alternative to the neoclassical approach is a way of opening the doors for new thinking and new practice. It should be added that this is not my first attempt but part of a life long professional story of looking for an economics more relevant to our time.

This book project was initiated in 2002 as part of activities financed by the European Union to strengthen regional cooperation for sustainable development. Reference was made to a 'Pan-European Regional Sustainable Development Network' with Wales as the lead region. How can actors in different regions, such as the Mälardalen region in Sweden (four counties, Stockholm included, in the valley of the lake Mälar) and Wales, learn about 'good practice' from each other? Cases of 'good practice' were presented from different regions and the idea was largely for network members to visit each other as part of an interactive learning process. Theoretical issues were not excluded but were, as I see it, left behind. The idea of different kinds of cooperation between regions – rather than nations – for sustainable development is certainly a good one but the tendency to focus directly on practice made me eventually lose contact with the network. My interest is rather in 'good theory' as a prerequisite for 'good practice'. Issues of paradigms in economics and development concepts with connected ideology have to be carefully addressed.

My early participation in the mentioned network made me reflect upon the European Union and regional (in the sense of sub-national) level of governance as part of this book project. But activities that may bring us closer to sustainability always begin at the level of the individual as actor and – as will be seen – my ideas about governance therefore tend to emphasize a view of humans as political economic persons acting in a society where democracy and governance are key considerations.

Peter Söderbaum
Västerås, February 2008

Acknowledgements

A book is not produced in a social vacuum. It is rather the result of continued dialogue with colleagues and students. Among colleagues, Eva Kras, Ralph Hall, Judy Brown, Cecilia Tortajada, Andrea Biswas, Edward Fullbrook, Magnus Linderström and an anonymous reviewer directly commented upon the text. Since the book aims not only at being a contribution to the international debate about economics and sustainability but also a textbook, I have asked two students, Lisa Grotkowski and Matthias Schröter from our international courses in Ecological Economics, Mälardalen University, to provide comments. Lisa Grotkowski and Ralph Hall have even suggested language improvements.

I also want to point to other persons who have played an important role in my development as an institutional and ecological economist. Among actors in the International Society for Ecological Economics from its beginning I would like to mention Kenneth Boulding, Herman Daly, Richard Norgaard, Juan Martinez-Alier, Clive Spash, Joachim Spangenberg, Malte Faber and Arild Vatn. As member of the scientific committee of Stockholm Water Symposium for a number of years I had the pleasure to cooperate with Malin Falkenmark, Asit Biswas, Jan Lundqvist and others. More recently Miriam Kennet and Volker Heinemann at the Green Economics Institute, UK, and Jack Reardon have been important.

The Ecological Economics group at Mälardalen University, Västerås, with Birgitta Schwartz, Kjell-Åke Brorsson, Peter Dobers, Malin Mobjörk, Karina Tilling, Anna Boman, Hans Lundberg, Ulf Johansson, Anders W. Johansson, Eva Friman (now at Uppsala University), Björn Forsberg (now at Umeå University) has been essential as have guests to this research group over the years: Tatiana Kluvánková-Oravská, Eva Cudlínová, Inge Röpke, Irina Glazyrina, Rajesvari S. Raina, and Mary E. Clark among others. Others who have strengthened and encouraged the institutionalization of ecological economics and sustainability issues at our university are Pekka Kuljunlahti and Elvy Westlund. Today Sustainable Development is accepted by Ingegerd Palmér, the President of the university, and other leading actors as an essential part of the university's profile. As an example, the previous School of Business has become part of a School of Sustainable Development of Society and Technology.

When writing a book, technical assistance to deal with computer problems is essential. Klas Andberger and Peter Falck have been extremely helpful. Lydia Haraldson at the City administration, Uppsala municipality, has assisted in illustrating one of the cases presented. At Earthscan, Rob West and Jonathan Sinclair Wilson have encouraged this book project from the very beginning. Production co-ordinator Hamish Ironside, copy-editor Elizabeth Riley, Alison Kuznets and Dan Harding have contributed in the final editing and marketing process.

It should be added that the present text is new but similar arguments have been presented in previous books, chapters in edited books and a number of articles, some mentioned in the list of references. This book is part of the outcome of a research project 'Actors, strategies, institutions: Cooperation for Sustainable Development' financed by The Swedish Research Council for Environment, Agricultural Sciences and Spatial Planning' (FORMAS), Stockholm. The contribution more recently by Paul Sjöblom, Marika Hedin and others at the Nobel Museum, Stockholm, for arranging seminars to critically illuminate the Bank of Sweden's Prize in Economic Sciences in Memory of Alfred Nobel is also acknowledged.

Last but not least I want to mention my wife Eva and our children Jakob, Simon, Ville and Hanna, and also three grandchildren, hoping that some of the unsustainable trends we see today will be dealt with in a constructive way.

Acronyms and Abbreviations

AAA	actor–agenda–arena
AFEE	Association for Evolutionary Economics
CAP	Common Agricultural Policy (of the EU)
CBA	cost–benefit analysis
CEO	chief executive officer
CLB	China Labour Bulletin
CO_2	carbon dioxide
CSR	corporate social responsibility
DIW	Deutsches Institut für Wirtschaftsforschung
DPSIR	drivers–pressures–states–impacts–responses
EAEPE	European Association for Evolutionary Political Economy
EEC	European Economic Community
EHM	economic hit man
EIA	environmental impact assessment
EMAS	Eco-Management and Auditing Scheme (of the EU)
EMS	environmental management system
EPI	environmental policy integration
ESEE	European Society for Ecological Economics
EU	European Union
GATT	General Agreement on Tariffs and Trade
GDP	gross domestic product
GEO	Global Environment Outlook
IAFFE	International Association for Feminist Economists
ICAPE	International Confederation of Associations for Pluralism in Economics
IJGE	*International Journal of Green Economics*
IMF	International Monetary Fund
ISEE	International Society for Ecological Economics
ISO	International Organization for Standardization
JOIE	*Journal of Institutional Economics*
LAC	Labour Action China
LCA	life cycle analysis
MBI	market-based instrument
MCA	multi-criteria approach
MDG	Millennium Development Goal

NE   neoclassical economics
NEM   neoclassical economic man
NEPA   National Environmental Policy Act
OECD   Organisation for Economic Co-operation and Development
PA   positional analysis
PAER   *Post-Autistic Economics Review*
PEO   political economic organization
PEP   political economic person
PPP   polluter pays principle
R&D   research and development
RLA   Right Livelihood Award
SAM   sustainability assessment model
SD   sustainable development
TABD   TransAtlantic Business Dialogue
UN   United Nations
UNDP   United Nations Development Programme
UNEP   United Nations Environment Programme
USD   unsustainable development
USR   university social responsibility
WBCSD   World Business Council for Sustainable Development
WCD   World Commission on Dams
WCED   World Commission on Environment and Development
WTO   World Trade Organization
WWF   World Wide Fund for Nature

Economics for Sustainability

When looked upon in traditional terms of international competitiveness and growth in gross domestic product (GDP), our economies may be performing well. But it is increasingly understood that this is not enough. Sometimes GDP growth goes together with environmental degradation. We hear about China and India, for instance, with growth rates of 8–9 per cent per year that are accompanied by worrying trends in environmental degradation. The success of one country in export markets may furthermore cause unemployment in other countries and increased exports may not even improve employment in the exporting country (as a result of improved labour productivity). Whatever the truth in specific countries, it has become clear for many of us that the performance of an economy has to be measured in multidimensional terms. Monetary indicators, such as GDP, exports, investments at the level of the national economy and monetary profits at the level of the business corporation are still of interest and relevant, but never enough. Limiting attention to monetary indicators can even be considered a dangerous strategy. It is like cutting off the branch one is sitting on by undermining the functioning of life-supporting systems for society at large.

This is where 'sustainability' has entered the scene as a broader idea of performance for the economy as a whole and for individuals and organizations at the micro level. Rather than focusing exclusively on economic growth, development has to become 'sustainable' according to a broad spectrum of indicators.

Sustainability as a contested concept

One traditional idea in science is that all concepts should be clearly defined and indicators should be chosen so that they can be measured in an undisputable way. This is probably one reason among many behind the emphasis on monetary indicators in economics. While the ambition to define and measure in a clear way is reasonable, we should at the same time learn to deal with some concepts that are not so clear and not so easily measured. Relying exclusively on easily measurable indicators in relation to complex societal issues would be a mistake. As argued by William Connolly (1993) in his study of political discourse, we should live with some 'contested concepts' and – it can be added

– this can be a way of opening the door for new thinking. While Connolly pointed to concepts such as 'politics', 'democracy', 'participation', 'power', 'freedom', 'legitimacy' and 'interest', it is here argued that 'sustainability' can also belong to this category. Actually, sustainability is just one in a long list of 'contested concepts' that is discussed in the present book. I also speak about broader theoretical approaches, so-called 'schools of thought' or paradigms as being contested, arguing that there are more perspectives than one.

In public debate and even scientific discourse one can find competing interpretations of 'sustainability'. As a scholar and citizen, I have preferences for specific ways of defining sustainability. Still, rather than excluding competing ideas from the beginning, I will deal with them and discuss more than one way of interpreting this term. Actually, an ideological power game is going on concerning the concept of sustainability and, as a social scientist, I find this power game interesting. Some politicians, established business actors and mainstream neoclassical economists may understand that apprehensions about climate change and other kinds of environmental degradation cannot easily be dismissed. However, there are those who vigorously defend a reliance on monetary indicators. In its simplest form this means that welfare in a society is connected with 'sustained economic growth' in GDP terms while success in business is a matter of 'sustained monetary profits'. Such 'monetary reductionism' (in the sense of attempting to reduce everything to its monetary aspect), while being common, is not unchallenged. 'Business as usual' is only one possible interpretation and, as I see it, it departs from the intentions of the World Commission on Environment and Development (WCED, 1987), the commission that launched the vision of sustainable development.

The vision of sustainable development: A short history

In 1972, a UN conference on the Human Environment was arranged in Stockholm. At this time, the relationship between human beings and the environment was not a new concern. Still, the Stockholm conference can be seen as one of the first systematic attempts to deal with the international dimensions of environmental degradation. Pollution problems, such as 'acid rain' and mercury contamination were among the many issues raised. Rachel Carson (1962), Barry Commoner (1971) and other natural scientists identified what is now referred to as unsustainable trends and the international community succeeded through the conference and along other paths to mitigate parts of the problems. Not only natural scientists but also economists, such as Ezra Mishan and Herman Daly, participated in the dialogue. Mishan's early book *The Costs of Economic Growth* (1967) suggests that ideas about progress emphasized in economics have to be reconsidered.

In everyday life and in science we too often simplify things. For instance, many actors argue and even believe that progress is equal to economic growth. Mishan's arguments, and those of many others, suggest that progress cannot be measured in one-dimensional monetary terms. We have to accept a degree of complexity. A multidimensional idea of progress is preferable and the habit of reducing all kinds of impacts to one dimension, whether money or some other unit, is rather part of the problems faced. Environmental impacts should be described and considered in their own terms and the same is true of the social, health and cultural aspects now considered part of the sustainability concept.

Sustainable development became a catchphrase with the release of the Brundtland report (WCED, 1987). Before its release much of the discourse was about perceived threats to the environment and natural resources. It was argued that economists have to take ecosystems seriously. Some suggested a focus on 'qualitative growth' rather than exclusively pointing to the quantitative monetary aspect (Leipert, 1983). Ignacy Sachs coined the term 'eco-development' in the sense of ecological development (Sachs, 1976, 1984) and in Eastern Europe, Hristo Marinov (1984), among others, argued in favour of 'ecologization of the economy'. Reference was made to 'ecological imperatives for public policy', i.e. principles for decision-making primarily formulated in negative terms (non-degradation of the natural resource base in your own region, non-degradation in other regions, observing a precautionary principle, etc.) (Söderbaum, 1980, 1982a).

In addition to multidimensional thinking as a way of broadening perspectives and interpretations, sustainable development involves a related effort to 'extend horizons' by bringing in ethics and ideology in a more explicit way. The idea here is that individuals should not limit their horizons to self-interest in a narrow sense and to immediate impacts. This political commitment means that the individual, in thinking and values, should step away from self-interest only, to include 'otherness' in the sense of internalizing the interest of others (Söderbaum, 2005). Such 'otherness' may refer to:

- the present generation of other individuals in the 'home' region;
- the present generation of individuals in other regions and ultimately in the global community;
- future generations of individuals in the home region;
- future generations of individuals in other regions and ultimately in the global community;
- present and future non-human forms of life.

The list can be extended. We can care about old landscapes, buildings and other cultural artefacts. Thinking in ethical terms is a way of bringing in the social aspects of sustainable development. Again, the important thing is to discuss social impacts in their own terms rather than in monetary terms. Welfare, poverty and human rights are multidimensional concepts and should not be reduced to some alleged monetary equivalent.

The above list may be perceived as overly idealistic – nobody can care about all other individuals in the home region and even less globally. Few of us would claim to consider all future generations in our decisions. The challenge is rather to get a feeling for the right direction and to get closer to sustainable development in a step-by-step fashion. We can ask ourselves, how can my lifestyle, in terms of market and non-market behaviour, be made more sustainable or less unsustainable? Similarly, actors in business corporations and other organizations, municipalities and national governments can broaden and extend their horizons in various ways. Policies and incentive systems formulated or designed by national governments can reflect visions of extended ethical horizons.

We all know that development patterns at the micro level – of individuals and organizations – or at the national and international levels are characterized by a lot of inertia and 'path-dependence'. Changing one's lifestyle with the purpose of reducing emissions of carbon dioxide (CO_2), for instance, is not easily done. The Rio de Janeiro conference in 1992, through its Agenda 21, pointed to a strengthening of democracy as the way ahead. Some changes in development patterns always occur in one direction or other and the challenge, from a sustainability point of view, is to add to positive changes and reduce the frequency of negative ones.

A short history of economic ideas

A critical question is whether we have an economic science that can constructively address sustainability problems of the kind indicated. Neoclassical economics (NE) is today the dominant paradigm in university departments of economics and in many other arenas where political dialogue takes place. What does 'neoclassical' stand for? Why this terminology? The prefix 'neo-' suggests that 'neoclassical' economists are the followers of 'classical' economists. The classical economists were active and dominant from the 18th century until about 1870, when the first generation of neoclassical economists entered the stage claiming some newness in their message.

Let us first broadly characterize the classical economists. Who were they? Textbooks in the history of economic ideas (for example Fusfeld, 1994) generally point to three people, Adam Smith, David Ricardo and Thomas Malthus. They were all broad-minded economists and philosophers who referred to their subject as 'political economics'. Adam Smith, who previously had contributed to moral philosophy, wrote his book *An Inquiry into the Nature and Causes of the Wealth of Nations* in 1776. Ricardo offered a theory about the claimed advantages of trade between nations and Malthus worried about the sufficiency of land (for food production) as a natural resource in relation to population growth.

Smith and Ricardo pointed to advantages of specialization or division of labour. These ideas even influenced the development pattern of science itself. Indeed, neoclassical economics from its very beginning, about 1870, is an example of this trend towards specialization. The idea was to get closer to a 'pure' science. Reference was made to 'economics' rather than 'political economics'. Neoclassical economists emphasized objectivity and value neutrality and wanted their discipline to be as close to physics as possible. Much like physics, they hoped to formulate universal principles and laws. This 'physics envy' made neoclassical economists emphasize analysis in terms of 'forces' (of supply and demand) leading to an 'equilibrium' and more generally, the use of a mathematical language.

So far, our story appears straightforward. First came the classical economists. Then the neoclassical economists emerged with the kind of economics that is still dominant in the Western world. This sounds, however, as if one paradigm is replacing the other and as if only one paradigm is regarded as valid at a time. In reality, tensions between different schools of thought in economics have always existed. One paradigm may be dominant but there have normally been competing views. Not all economists became enthusiastic about the claimed advances of Karl Menger, William Stanley Jevons, Léon Walras and others in the first generation of neoclassical economists. The German Historical School around 1850 and later the American institutionalists, with Thorstein Veblen, John R. Commons and Weslie Mitchell, followed a different path and understood economics in evolutionary terms (Dorfman et al, 1964; Fusfeld, 1994, pp95–99).

Among more recent institutional economists who took an interest in environmental and development issues are K. William Kapp (1950), the first modern ecological economist (see also Martinez-Alier, 1999), and Gunnar Myrdal (1972, 1978), one of the pioneers of holistic and interdisciplinary development studies. In spite of systematic discrimination of non-neoclassical economists at the universities, a number of competing organizations have been strengthened and institutionalized. Among associations for institutionalists, the US-based Association for Evolutionary Economics (AFEE) with the *Journal of Economic Issues*, and the European Association for Evolutionary Political Economy (EAEPE), with the more recent *Journal of Institutional Economics* (JOIE), can be mentioned.

This story is admittedly short but I will come back to the meaning of neoclassical economics and comparisons with institutional economics repeatedly. One more point deserves attention at this stage: I believe it was a serious mistake by the neoclassical economists to abandon the label 'political'. Neoclassical theory reflects a specific ideological and political orientation. Similarly, institutional economics and other competing schools of thought are specific in ideological terms. In fact, the reason why an economist prefers a specific paradigm or theoretical perspective is usually scientific *and* ideological.[1]

Tenets of neoclassical economics

Since neoclassical economics will be scrutinized in the pages to follow, it is useful to first summarize several salient features of neoclassical economics. It is up to the reader to judge whether the neoclassical way of understanding the economy or economics is ideologically neutral or not.

NE is a relatively coherent theoretical perspective. Some of its fundamental assumptions can be described as follows:

- The actors considered in NE are 'firms' and 'consumers'.
- Firms and consumers are related to each other through 'markets' for commodities (goods and services) and markets for 'factors of production' (labour, capital, natural resources).
- There is also a role for the 'national government' as a regulator of markets, to administer taxation and to make decisions about how tax income should be used.
- Markets (for commodities and factors of production) are understood mechanistically in terms of 'supply' and 'demand'.
- The 'economy' consists of the mentioned actor categories and their market relationships.
- The interests of consumers (consumer preferences) and firms (monetary profit) are assumed to be given.
- Assumed self-interest is the starting point for the consumer's and firm's calculations of optimal behaviour.
- The consumer is assumed to be maximizing utility subject to a budget constraint and the firm is maximizing monetary profits (i.e. the difference between revenues and costs for each period).
- Decision-making is understood as systematic comparison of alternatives, observing the so-called 'opportunity cost principle'. Reasoning in marginal terms is common: what will be the benefits and costs of producing (purchasing) one extra unit of a specific commodity?
- Efficiency at the national level is understood in terms of a monetary analysis of 'costs' and 'benefits', so-called cost–benefit analysis (CBA).
- GDP is regarded as the main indicator of the 'health' of an economy.

Environmental economics is essentially an extension of NE and follows the same logic. It is recognized that there are some environmental problems. They are connected with so-called 'externalities' (i.e. impacts on third parties, parties not being part of a market transaction). The idea is then that negative impacts on third parties should be internalized (to become part of the market transaction) and the 'polluter pays principle' (PPP) observed. When the market fails, this failure should then be corrected. It is similarly argued that governments may fail. For example, governments may financially support activities (of firms and consumers) that systematically contribute to the degradation of the environment.

The 'physics envy' aspect of neoclassical economics suggests additional features: first, NE relies heavily on positivism as a theory of science, and second, NE emphasizes mathematics as the language of presentation.

More recent advances in the theory of science are connected with the humanities and social sciences. These theories, such as social constructivism and hermeneutics, are largely neglected. The preference for presentation in mathematical terms is another self-imposed limitation to the approach.

In ideological terms, NE can be described as a specific market ideology, downplaying or excluding other market and non-market ideologies. In fact, NE plays an important role as a conceptual framework and ideology, legitimizing the present kind of market or corporate capitalism. One question is whether the ideology of market capitalism inherent in neoclassical economics will bring us in the direction of a sustainable economy or not (O'Connor, 1994). Is there another kind of 'capitalism' with a better chance of responding to the sustainability challenge?

Neoclassical economics as narrative

To get a feeling for how things are related to each other, I will present neoclassical economics as a narrative:

> *Life is essentially about consumption. The higher your income, the more you can consume. Your preferences for consumer goods and services are a private matter and you should choose the bundle of commodities that maximizes your utility.*
>
> *The role of firms (business companies) is to produce goods and services for consumption. This should be done in ways that maximize monetary profits. No conflict of interest exists within the company and there should be no limit to the rights of firms to exploit natural resources and penetrate markets in all parts of the world. Profits can be accumulated to further strengthen the power position of the company and its shareholders.*

> *The exchange of goods and services is mechanistically regulated in markets through the forces of supply and demand. Competition generally reduces prices so that consumers can buy more commodities for a given income, adding to their welfare.*
>
> *The monetary value of commodities exchanged in the market in a country during a year, the GDP, will tell us about the happiness or welfare of the inhabitants of that country. The success of an economy can thus be measured in monetary terms (as increase in GDP compared with last year) and compared with the performance of other countries. Projects, programmes and policies can similarly be compared and evaluated in monetary terms using CBA, where the present value of each project can be estimated. Politicians need simple and clear indicators. People are used to and can understand the language of money.*

This story is simplified and points to negative features in a way that can be labelled cynical. But it nevertheless contains some of the main ideas or ways of thinking in neoclassical economics.

Recent demand for alternatives to neoclassical economics

While neoclassical economics has been criticized over the years, it still holds a strong position. Among alternatives to neoclassicism, institutional economics will be emphasized in this book. There are also other schools of thought that question the dominance, if not monopoly, of the neoclassical paradigm at departments of economics all over the world. There is an Association for Social Economics with the *Review of Social Economy* as a first example. There is an International Association for Feminist Economists (IAFFE, www.iaffe.org) with its journal *Feminist Economics* and contributions in this field may refer to 'neoclassical feminist economics' or 'non-neoclassical feminist economics' (see also Ferber and Nelson, 1993). In both cases, the assumed value or ideological orientation of women represents a starting point. The International Society for Ecological Economics (ISEE), with the journal *Ecological Economics*, is pluralistic (Norgaard, 1989) in the sense that non-neoclassical as well as neoclassical economists are members. This society must tread carefully to manage its delicate balance in a world of neoclassical dominance.

To get an overview of the many claimed alternatives to orthodoxy, the *Heterodox Economics Newsletter* (www.heterodoxnews.com) and the *Post-Autistic Economics Review* (PAER) can be interrogated (www.paecon.net). The latter review is a manifestation of a protest movement that began at French universities in 2000 (Fullbrook, 2003). Students questioned the 'autistic' nature of lectures and textbooks in economics and asked for alternatives of a 'post-autistic' kind. The French minister of education initiated an investigation. Some professors of economics in different parts of the world responded to the call for change and have contributed in various ways, for instance in books edited by Edward Fullbrook (2003, 2004, 2007). It may be of interest to note that the book from 2003 has been translated into Chinese.[2]

Another recent sign of a crack in the neoclassical defence lines is a call for an 'economics for sustainability' by the German federal government and its Ministry of Education and Research. Neoclassical economics was judged 'inadequate' in relation to present sustainability challenges. One of the established neoclassical economics institutes, Deutsches Institut für Wirtschaftsforschung (DIW), Berlin, was asked to initiate a series of workshops to address the new challenge (www.sustainabilityeconomics.de). Ecological economists with non-neoclassical worldviews participated to assess the state of 'sustainability economics'. In the UK, focusing on the role of economics, a Green Economics Institute (www.greeneconomics.org.uk) has been formed with a connected *International Journal of Green Economics* (IJGE).

In conclusion, it can be argued that there are many alternatives to neoclassical economics and that for some of the alternatives common features can be easily listed. Opening the door for pluralism at university departments of economics is a big challenge. The International Confederation of Associations for Pluralism in Economics (ICAPE) (www.icape.org) is a society for this purpose.

A comparative and pluralistic approach

The approach of the present book can be described as comparative in the sense that elements of institutional economics are systematically compared to corresponding elements of neoclassical economics. Alternatives to the neoclassical view of individuals, organizations, markets, international trade, progress in society, decision-making, social and institutional change processes, etc. will be given. Some readers may find this comparative analysis tiresome or unnecessary. They may welcome a positive message but feel that criticism should be limited or excluded.

Contrary to this view, I believe that criticism plays an essential role in the academy and in society at large. It is a way of learning. The kind of criticism voiced should here be seen as part of the pluralistic strategy. No paradigm or theoretical perspective can claim universal applicability, i.e. usefulness for all kinds of problems. Each paradigm or theoretical perspective may have something to offer and preference for one theoretical perspective over another is –

as we have seen – partly a matter of ideology. The thing to be criticized is rather pretensions for the monopoly of one particular paradigm.

Milton Friedman, one of the neoclassical economists, has written much about 'freedom' and refers to a kind of freedom in the market place for some categories of actors (Friedman and Friedman, 1980). A more fundamental freedom that is not part of Friedman's ideological message is the 'freedom of thought'. No single person or collective of economists can claim monopoly with respect to conceptual framework or a right to exclude other storylines about economics at universities. Furthermore, if economics is about 'choice', why should one accept dictatorship with respect to theoretical perspective?

Scientific development is not exclusively a competition between one clear-cut paradigm versus another. It is a more complex process where each theoretical perspective gradually changes and new mixtures or combinations of theoretical elements or perspectives emerge. Familiarity with more than one theoretical perspective will add to our understanding and opportunities for constructive research.

As a way of summarizing, it can be argued that 'learning by comparison' is a good idea at both the level of practice and when learning about and further developing conceptual frameworks and theories. In considering the purchase of a new bicycle, car or refrigerator, many of us compare the features of the product with something that we already know about, for example our present bicycle, car or refrigerator. Similarly, when 'buying' a new conceptual framework, it might be a good idea to compare the new framework with one that people are acquainted with.

Notes

1   'Ideology' is here used in a broad sense to refer to ideas about means–ends relationship and is not limited to established political ideologies, such as liberalism or social democracy.
2   Ecological economics and economics for sustainability in relation to China are discussed by Shi (2002a, 2002b).

Further readings

Sustainability economics can be described as economics for sustainable development or economics for sustainability. It represents a broad interpretation of ecological economics where environmental and ecological variables and issues are basic but part of a multidimensional perspective. Social, cultural, health-related and monetary/financial aspects have to be integrated into the analysis. As indicated in the text, sustainable development as a concept and buzzword is very much connected with the Brundtland report (WCED, 1987). One early ecological economics text that has been quite influential is *For the Common Good. Redirecting the Economy Toward Community, the Environment and a Sustainable Future* by Herman Daly and John Cobb (1989). Thomas Prugh, Robert Costanza and Herman Daly later wrote a textbook in ecological economics, *The Local Politics of Global Sustainability* (Prugh et al, 2000). For a multifaceted and historical account of social theories in relation to nature and environment, see *Environment and Social Theory* by John Barry (2007).

A second theme in this book concerns economics in more general terms. It is an attempt to develop institutional theory as an alternative to mainstream neoclassical economics and at the same time a plea for pluralism in economics. Among early critics of neoclassical economics, K. William Kapp and Gunnar Myrdal are mentioned in the main text with their books *The Social Costs of Private Enterprise* (1950) and *Against the Stream. Critical Essays on Economics* (1972), respectively. Both saw themselves as institutional economists.

For those not so well acquainted with neoclassical theory, a textbook in microeconomics is recommended. While texts in microeconomics are quite similar and can largely be regarded as homogeneous commodities, it should be observed that there is also some prudent criticism from within the mainstream. Amartya Sen's *On Ethics and Economics* (1987) is an example of this. He is critical of the almost exclusive reliance on an 'engineering tradition' where ethical aspects more or less disappear. He recommends a development path for economics where ethics is taken seriously.

Question for discussion

➤ Mainstream neoclassical economics has been described in Chapter 1 in an admittedly negative manner. This may be considered unfair but the idea is to uncover some of the essential assumptions behind the approach and thereby specific scientific and ideological features. Is neoclassical economics only about science and truth in a value-neutral sense or do you agree that ideology is involved? If the latter is the case – how can one deal with this understanding?

2

Unsustainable and Sustainable Trends

In Chapter 1, sustainable development (SD) was described as a 'contested concept'. One option is to leave it like that and happily point to the confusion that exists: 'We do not need to bother about this obscure idea of sustainability'. Another option, and the one that is chosen here, is to try to identify competing interpretations of SD and then reject some interpretations in favour of others. Attempts will then be made to broadly define what I see as the more constructive interpretations of SD. A direction of desired social and institutional change will hopefully emerge. Such decisions about definitions and direction of desired change are, as I have argued, ethical, ideological and political.

The next issue is one of measurement. Having pointed in a specific direction, how can one distinguish between progress (i.e. desired development) and its opposite, degradation? How can sustainability be measured? Are there trends that are clearly 'unsustainable' and others that are 'sustainable'? What indicators can be used? Can the search for useful indicators be guided by some general principles?

Sustainability issues are relevant at all levels from the individual to organizations (of a business or other nature) to municipalities, cities and regions, such as the Mälardalen region or the EU. Readers will rely on their own experiences to find empirical examples. To facilitate the learning process, empirical examples of efforts to counteract unsustainable trends will be discussed in this chapter: the UN Millennium Development Goals (MDGs), environmental policy in the EU, efforts in Sweden to formulate environmental quality objectives and finally city planning in my own municipality, Uppsala.

Competing interpretations of sustainable development

All kinds of measures to improve environmental and social performance at different levels – from the individual to the group and organization to local, regional and national authorities and ultimately the global level – should be encouraged. Small changes in the direction of a more sustainable society could be part of more radical transformation processes. However, the obstacles in front of us should not be underestimated since many individuals as actors stick to traditional ideas of progress. I will make an admittedly simplified distinction between three ideological orientations – with connected response patterns – in relation to environment and development. Individuals as actors may feel that they belong both in rhetoric and practice to one category or that they are somehow divided between categories. An external observer may judge the individual differently from the individual's self-assessment. The three orientations are:

1   'Business as usual' – according to actors who embrace this ideological orientation, statements about the existence of environmental and social problems are generally exaggerated. To the extent that such problems exist, it is believed that they can easily be handled within the scope of a continued emphasis on economic growth, technological innovations and global market penetration. No change in dominant paradigm, ideology or institutional framework is needed. The response pattern is: 'If we do not speak about the problems, then perhaps they do not exist'; 'To the extent that they exist, they will be taken care of by the inbuilt mechanisms of our present market economy'; 'Public relations campaigns and lobbying will make people focus on traditional parameters such as economic growth and profits thereby forgetting about environmental problems'.

2   'Social and ecological modernization' (c.f., Hajer, 1995) – those who hold this ideological orientation or worldview share a judgement that humanity faces environmental and social problems of a serious and, in some respects, new kind. There are some unsustainable trends that have to be tackled. In all organizations, management systems have to be modified to allow for this new situation. It is recognized that action is needed at all levels from the individual to the organization, to the local and national government, to the global level. But presently dominant paradigms, ideologies (in business and elsewhere) and institutional framework need only be modified and 'modernized' to allow for the new situation. Environmental economics as an extension of neoclassical economics, with PPP will do it. The response pattern is therefore: 'Yes, there are problems but don't worry, things are under control'; 'Environmental taxes, trade in pollution permits and other market instruments can be used, codes of conduct for corporations will be formulated'; 'Voluntary agreements between business corporations and environmental organizations, environmental management systems, environmental labelling etc. will do it'.

3   'Radical interpretation of SD' – those who hold this view or ideological orientation identify unsustainable trends and argue that major shifts in paradigm, ideology and institutional framework have to be seriously considered as part of a pluralistic strategy. Modifying the presently dominant paradigm, ideology and institutional framework may get us closer to an SD path but will not be enough. SD as an ideological orientation has to be taken seriously, and a major shift in thinking is essential. The response

pattern is: 'We need complementary or alternative conceptual frameworks in economics and science more generally as part of a pluralistic and democratic philosophy'; 'Competition is preferred to the global neoclassical monopoly or cartel at university departments of economics'; 'Individuals and organizations alike need to reconsider their ideas about progress as actors privately, professionally and in society'; 'Institutional arrangements at the local, national and international level are too often dysfunctional in relation to sustainability objectives'.

The 'business as usual' attitude is exemplified by an advertising campaign by the Confederation of Swedish Enterprise (May 2002), where welfare is exclusively connected with economic growth in GDP and the main concern is Sweden's position in GDP terms when compared with other countries in a 'welfare league'. It is seen as a big problem, overshadowing all other concerns that 'Sweden is lagging behind'. Not one word is written about the environment or broader ideas about welfare and economics, such as SD. This particular trade organization does not completely neglect the debate about SD, a person is in fact employed to take care of these issues. However, judging from their website and advertising, SD is not a big issue for them.[1]

Our second ideological orientation, 'ecological modernization' is described by Maarten Hajer (1995, p31, p32, p25) as follows:

> *Ecological modernization… uses the language of business and conceptualizes environmental pollution as a matter of inefficiency, while operating within the boundaries of cost-effectiveness and administrative efficiency.*

> *Ecological modernization explicitly avoids addressing basic social contradictions. [It] does not call for any structural change but is, in this respect, basically a modernist and technocratic approach to the environment that suggests that there is a technological-institutional fix for the present problems.*

> *In the most general terms ecological modernization can be defined as the discourse that recognizes the structural character of the environmental problematique but none the less assumes that existing political, economic, and social institutions can internalize the care for the environment.*

Behind some of the present 'political, economic, and social institutions' mentioned by Hajer is neoclassical economics as a legitimizing paradigm. Negative externalities, i.e. impacts on third parties, should be internalized with reference to PPP. Taxes and charges can be used to allow for such costs. Implicit in this argument is the idea that only minor adjustments are needed.

The ideological orientation of the World Business Council for Sustainable Development (WBCSD) exemplifies an organization that is close to the ideology of ecological modernization. According to its home page (www.wbcsd.org, accessed 13 July 2006):

> *WBCSD brings together some 180 international companies in a shared commitment to sustainable development through economic growth, ecological balance and social progress.*
>
> *We must recast the debate away from the perceived conflict between shareholder value and corporate social responsibility. While the fundamental role of business will always be creating value, the boundaries that divide the role of business from those of governments and non-governmental organizations are blurring and shifting. Our major contributions will come through our core business, not through philanthropic programs. If action to address global issues is to be substantial and sustainable, it must be profitable.*
>
> *Business must play an ever-more effective role in managing these issues through partnerships and new business models. Key to this will be building trust in order to enhance support for business's main purpose: to generate wealth, jobs, innovations and investments. Business cannot succeed in a society that fails.*

WBCSD is what later will be referred to as a 'political economic organization' that participates in public debate about sustainability and other development issues. It also engages in lobbying activities in relation to national governments and international organizations. While there is a commitment to sustainability, there is, at the same time, a more fundamental commitment to economic growth, monetary profits and shareholder value. Climate change is regarded as a threat but this is used as a pretext for advocating nuclear power, notwithstanding the well-known environmental problems connected with this energy source. In my understanding, the sustainability rhetoric is supposed to further strengthen a traditional role of market expansion for trans-national companies. This subjective interpretation does not exclude the possibility that there are actors connected with the WBCSD arena that interpret sustainability in a more radical way.

Proponents of our third ideological orientation, 'radical interpretation of SD', imply a major shift in paradigm, ideology and institutional framework.

They can be found in many professions. This orientation is perhaps best associated with civil society organizations, for instance the French Attac movement with actors such as Susan George (2000) and René Passet (2000). George and Passet both point to neo-liberalism and neoclassical economics as part of the problem. The same is true of David Korten in his book *When Corporations Rule the World* (2001). Feministic perspectives add to our understanding (Shiva, 2002, 2005) and also fiction writers may provide a different conceptual and ideological perspective in relation to specific issues, such as dam construction (Roy, 2001). Persons who combine scientific knowledge with journalism can similarly make the behaviour of various actors on the local or international scenes more visible. This is exemplified by Jeremy Legget's study of climate change negotiations (1999) and John Humphrys's exposé of agricultural, food and health policy (2001).

While there is some room for the third, more radical, interpretation of SD, actors with 'business as usual' or 'ecological modernization' attitudes tend to dominate in many arenas. Trans-national companies and politicians with a neo-liberal orientation have been successful for some time in defining problems and influencing the development dialogue. There is even a tendency that the traditional idea of business being regulated by national government (and through international agreements between national governments) has been replaced in favour of a situation where business has some influence in controlling and 'regulating' national governments. The TransAtlantic Business Dialogue (TABD) (www.tabd.com) is an example of this trend. Trans-national corporations based in the US or EU claim specific rights to accept or not accept political proposals that concern them and also have specific channels to the US government and administration and the Commission of the EU, respectively.

Giving more power to business organizations that are essentially governed by monetary principles will neither give us a sustainable society at the regional level nor at the global level and is hardly in the interest of business. At some stage, more power to businesses may even undermine the power of business itself. A global world ruled by the international business community is for some of us not much better than the Soviet type of planned economies of the past. Our democracy is based on a division of power and does not permit any coalition of organizations to take over leadership and control. In the recent past we have seen cases of failure and mismanagement by 'big business'. This has led to reactions by civil society in different parts of the world.

It would be a mistake to believe that business is the only culprit, and to make general statements about all business leaders and all kinds of companies. In relation to a specific actor category, such as business leaders, the 'heterogeneity principle' applies. Proponents of what we have called a radical interpretation of SD may be found in any category of actors and also among professionals in business. Significant differences can be expected for instance between actors in trans-national corporations and in small locally operating companies. Similarly, universities as organizations, and scholars or other professionals at universities, differ in their ideological orientation. A lot remains to be done at universities before one can claim that environmental and development issues are taken seriously. The 'business as usual' attitude can be as common in university circles as elsewhere.

Towards a 'reasonable' interpretation of SD

As indicated in Chapter 1, SD became a catchphrase with the Brundtland report (WCED, 1987) and the Rio de Janeiro conference in 1992. Since then it has been repeated in a number of governmental and other documents at national and international levels. In relation to each one of these documents (or agreements), one option is to try to interpret it correctly. What did the authors of the document and the signatories mean when pointing to SD as a guiding principle?

One difficulty with the 'correct interpretation approach' is that some of the documents, such as the Brundtland report, are not very clear and they may even be contradictory in their arguments. Traditional ideas about economic growth (even 'vigorous economic growth') are presented side by side with pleas for strengthened environmental protection. A possible and probable explanation is that authors who contributed to the text significantly differed with respect to their ideological orientations.

Another difficulty is that for a given entity, such as the Swedish government or the EU, there are several agreements and documents. In the case of the EU, the Lisbon strategy emphasizes sustained economic growth and international competitiveness (European Council, 2000) while being relatively silent about environmental and related sustainability issues. The latter are dealt with in other EU declarations and strategies connected with the cities of Cardiff (Commission of the European Communities, 1998) and Gothenburg (European Council, 2001). The Cardiff meeting precedes the Lisbon strategy and emphasizes the principle of environmental policy integration (Lenschow, 2002),[2] whereas the Gothenburg meeting can be seen as an attempt to correct or modify some of the statements from Lisbon. It appears that actors in leading EU positions can choose whatever strategy they prefer and so far traditional objectives of growth and trade appear to be the highest priority. The present (October 2007) EU Commissioner for trade, Peter Mandelson, and the former Swedish Minister of Trade, Thomas Östros, exemplify actors who, in 2006, in World Trade Organization (WTO) negotiations and in other arenas, argued as if growth through increased international trade is their only vision. The mental maps and ideological orientations of Mandelson and Östros appear to be limited to neoclassical economics, and in particular, international trade theory.[3]

The ideological orientation of Mandelson and Östros is not difficult to understand considering the history of the EU. The Rome Treaty and the early customs union with six countries were based on ideas about 'economic integration' and the same was true of the European Economic Community (EEC). Commercial and other benefits from trade were emphasized while, for example, information about negative impacts of increased transportation was downplayed and only reluctantly published (Task Force Environment and the Internal Market, 1990).

While inertia and path-dependence may explain essential parts of the present functioning of the EU, it is increasingly recognized that something new is needed to cope with present sustainability challenges. Considering the difficulties of the mentioned 'correct interpretation approach', I have chosen to look for a 'reasonable' interpretation of SD. I will pick up some ideas that appear to have credibility in many circles and then add my own thoughts about the subject. In this manner existing political agreements and documents are regarded as elements in an ongoing search process.

In my own (admittedly ideological) interpretation, SD as a catchphrase is opposed to simplistic ideas about economic growth, etc. This implies that the 'business as usual' strategy is not expected to work for sustainability purposes. Local, national and regional communities are facing threats and challenges that are, in some respects, new. The 'newness' of SD as a development concept and ideological orientation refers to an increased emphasis on four key points. These are:

1   non-monetary impacts, especially unsustainable trends of different kinds to be counteracted;
2   security issues (prevention, precautionary principle, etc.);
3   ethical issues (intra-generational, inter-generational and in relation to non-human forms of life), 'from self-interest alone to also include common interests';
4   emphasis on democracy, governance and capacity building to make the above change in direction possible.

Implicit in the plea for SD is the idea that 'unsustainable development' (USD) should be avoided. Unsustainable trends of different kinds are identified and counteracted. The question is what kind of trends one should focus on. According to some, sustainability is a matter of three aspects: environmental, social and economic. In business jargon, reference is often made to a 'triple bottom line' (Zadek, 2001; Savitz and Weber, 2006) as opposed to a single bottom line in monetary terms. In the more constructive part of the EU discourse, the environmental aspect is often connected with the health aspect, for example the sixth environment action programme of the European

Community (Commission of the European Communities, 2001a) and some add culture as another part of SD. I will suggest that this broad thinking should potentially include all kinds of elements in a multidimensional analysis.

While monetary aspects of development are still relevant and of interest, the newness with SD is that it increases the emphasis on non-monetary aspects of development and has the idea that non-monetary factors and impacts should be understood in their own terms, as opposed to being reduced to some alleged monetary equivalent. The fact that money plays a role in many activities should not lead us to the conclusion that all other aspects can be understood, assessed and easily handled in monetary terms.

Rather than limiting ourselves to the three categories (i.e. environmental, social and economic) defined in some way, we can list a larger number of aspects or dimensions. Impacts of a policy, programme or project may refer to:

- ecological and environmental dimensions;
- health dimensions;
- social dimensions (concerning human rights, equality, monetary and non-monetary aspects of poverty, 'fairness', 'justice', etc.);
- cultural dimensions;
- aesthetic dimensions;
- financial and monetary dimensions.

In addition there are dimensions of a more comprehensive kind:

- dimensions related to knowledge and experience gained;
- dimensions related to power, ideology and ethics;
- legal and institutional dimensions.

The importance of each category is a matter of political choice and cannot be answered by science alone. Science can point to some of the features of each dimension, as I discuss later. Are impacts of a specific kind largely irreversible? Will future generations suffer if we make a specific choice of a policy or project?

Habits of thought connected with neoclassical economics suggest that every impact has a price in monetary terms and that all kinds of impacts can be traded against each other. David Pearce, among neoclassical environmental economists, understands that some impacts on natural resources are irreversible but nevertheless refers to a 'total economic value' in monetary terms, which is the sum of 'actual use value', 'option value' and 'existence value' (Pearce et al, 1989, p62). Other actors belonging to the same tradition try to respond to present challenges by referring to additional kinds of 'capital', such as 'human capital' and 'social capital' (Dasgupta and Serageldin, 2000). Such ideas about 'total economic value' or 'total capital' (as the sum of all kinds of capital) by reference to 'correct market prices' become a bit strained when markets do not exist. Should we rely on neoclassical experts who in mysterious ways refer to hypothetical markets? Even if actual markets existed, are they at all relevant to the kind of ideological issues we are facing? Arguing that all markets affected will point to prices that are ethically 'fair' is an ideological position that one may share or question. The proposal here is to avoid aggregating impacts. Instead, one should illuminate an issue in multidimensional and profile terms. This is a theme that is resumed in the pages to follow.

The connotations connected with the term 'capital' tend to point in a monetary direction for many of us. But 'capital' may also be understood in a qualitative sense and some of those who refer to human capital or social capital, such as Elinor Ostrom, are open to broader interpretations (Ostrom, 2000). As I see it, there is still some tendency to try and turn complexity into simplicity by referring to everything as capital. A citation from Gareth Morgan and his book *Images of Organization* (1986, p16) may be relevant here:

> *We live in a world that is becoming increasingly complex. Unfortunately our styles of thinking rarely match this complexity. We often end up persuading ourselves that everything is more simple than it actually is, dealing with complexity by presuming that it does not really exist.*

If reality is complex, then one has to live with this complexity or at least a considerable part of it rather than assume it away. The existence of 'complexity' is closely connected with incompleteness of knowledge and information, and therefore uncertainty. We are close to our second point of suggesting some newness in SD as ideological orientation, i.e. security issues and a focus on prevention and the precautionary principle. Here it can be argued that traditional development concepts in terms of GDP-growth have often been connected with extreme forms of technological optimism: 'Technology will solve all kinds of problems. It may take some time but...'. We now know that technological research and development (R&D) can be very helpful indeed. At the same time, a more prudent attitude is called for. Problems, such as climate change, storage of hazardous radioactive waste or chemical contamination can be mitigated but not easily solved. Increasing monetary investments in R&D may or may not get us closer to a sustainable society in these cases. A precautionary principle appears relevant. The tendency to instead downplay evidence about toxicological and other health and environmental problems has been documented by Poul Harremoës et al (2002) in a study for the European Environment Agency. Among cases where early warnings have not been taken seriously are fisheries, radiation, benzene, asbestos, PCBs (polychlorinated biphenyls), halocarbons, hormones as growth promoters and so-called 'mad cow disease'.

Security issues can hardly be dealt with these days without considering violence and terrorism. Will one interpretation of sustainability be preferable to another in reducing tensions and the number of terrorist attacks? Here, once more, an orientation in development thinking towards equality, fairness and justice appears to be a good choice. Something other than neo-liberalism and neoclassical economics is needed.

In the third point about the newness of sustainability as a development concept, reference was made to the need to articulate and illuminate ethical issues – from exclusive focus on self-interest (as in neoclassical economics) to also include common interests. The title of the Brundtland report *Our Common Future* (WCED, 1987) points to this.

Human beings as actors in different roles do not easily change their behaviour. However, small changes in visions and actions occur all the time and why shouldn't the positive changes towards sustainability dominate? Such changes will lead to institutional change processes that in turn will facilitate further change in visions and action. Reference can perhaps be made to a non-monetary multiplier effect (as distinguished from the neoclassical monetary 'multiplier effects'). Starting at the level of local communities, individuals can internalize some values as 'global citizens' (and not only act as consumers and business professionals that are supposed to gain from participation in a global market economy).

The fourth point listed as having the potential to renew the development dialogue focuses on democracy. In some sense and to some extent, democracy already exists in many countries. Still, it can be strengthened everywhere. SD is a challenge for all countries and calls for interactive learning processes where all individuals and all kinds of organizations can potentially contribute. Professionals and citizens alike have a lot to learn and they can learn from each other. This is an issue that I will return to.

Principles for multidimensional measurement: Thinking in non-monetary and positional terms

In Table 2.1 a classification of impacts is suggested. A distinction is made between impacts that are expressed in monetary terms and those described or measured in non-monetary terms. A second distinction refers to time. Are impacts (monetary or non-monetary) expressed as flows (referring to periods of time) or as positions or states (referring to points in time)? This leaves us with four categories of impacts: monetary flows ('a' in Table 2.1), monetary positions (category 'b'), non-monetary flows (category 'c') and non-monetary positions (category 'd').

Table 2.1 *Categories of impact in economic analysis*

	Flow (referring to a period of time)	Position (referring to a point in time)
Monetary	a	b
Non-monetary	c	d

At the level of the national economy, GDP exemplifies a monetary flow (category 'a'), the financial debt of the national treasury at the end of a year a monetary position (category 'b'), pollution of CO_2 into the atmosphere during a year a non-monetary flow ('c') and a country's land use for urban purposes in hectares at the end of a year a non-monetary position ('d').

At the level of organizations, for example a business company, the turnover in monetary terms in a year is a monetary flow, the market value of the company's assets at the end of a year is a monetary position, pollution of mercury from a factory in a year to a nearby lake is a non-monetary flow and parts per million (ppm) of mercury in fish caught in the same lake at a particular point in time is a non-monetary position.

At the level of an individual, the salary received per month is a monetary flow and the debts of the person at a point in time a monetary position. The amount of petrol used by the person per month when driving a car is a non-monetary flow, and the know-how and knowledge of a person at a point in time is a non-monetary position.

Obviously, there is an interaction over time between monetary flows and monetary positions, and between non-monetary flows and non-monetary positions in specific dimensions. Non-monetary impacts are similarly related to monetary ones.

Why are non-monetary impacts so important? Why is it not enough to focus on the monetary aspect? The answer is a matter of common sense. The monetary dimension is just one among dimensions and it is a strange idea that all other dimensions can be reduced to money or even that it is meaningful to try to reduce as many dimensions as possible to money. But neoclassical ideology and business propaganda have made many of us believe that economics is about money and that management of all kinds of resources is best handled in monetary or market terms. Given such habits of thought one has to approach this issue in a step-by-step manner. In this way, the dogma of exclusively monetary reasoning is questioned.

There are different types of non-monetary factors, processes and impacts. Ecological processes differ from social processes, etc. It is a trivial observation that we, as human beings, largely see the world through non-monetary lenses and that expected non-monetary impacts are essential in our decision-making.

For some subcategories of decisions, markets, prices and other monetary considerations are not invoked at all.

In other cases, the monetary aspect is essential and it carries with it a 'trading philosophy' – 'everything has a price', 'an impact can be traded against another in monetary terms'. It is here argued that this kind of thinking is simplistic and quite limited even in relation to market transactions. There are non-monetary aspects of transactions that should be made visible rather than hidden as part of a price or monetary cost. (The 'cost' of building a highway on agricultural and forest land is not limited to the monetary construction costs. Non-monetary aspects of this irreversible process have to be made visible and dealt with separately. While reference is often made to a 'construction' process, elements of 'destruction' are necessarily involved.) The reason for this is that non-monetary factors and impacts have their own logic, different from the mentioned trading philosophy.

Concepts such as inertia, path-dependence and irreversibility play a central role for factors related to ecology (or environment), health, social and cultural issues (i.e. the kind of aspects included in the concept of sustainability). In relation to irreversible damage to ecosystems (for example biodiversity loss), reference to correct prices and trading breaks down and a new accounting philosophy is needed (see for example Brown, 2000). Other examples are given in the pages to follow.

It is here argued that progress or lack of progress towards sustainability (and welfare, for that matter) is best described in non-monetary, positional terms. Is the health of an individual or a population of human beings improving or not from one point in time to another? Is the health of an ecosystem improving or deteriorating between two points in time? Is the availability and quality of drinking water at a particular place improving or being degraded between two points in time?

Monetary thinking tends to carry with it an idea that calculation is always possible. In reality, uncertainty and incompleteness of information may make such calculations less meaningful. A chess analogy may illustrate this point. In chess, as in life more generally, decisions are taken in multiple steps. In comparing alternative first-step moves, calculation – and even less, monetary calculation – is probably not very meaningful. Each alternative will lead to a new qualitative position of the chessmen on the board and new options or opportunities follow. Each move is irreversible in the sense that the player is not permitted to undo a particular move. The chance of success is a matter of thinking in visual patterns rather than numbers. I return to this thinking in terms of multiple steps when presenting positional analysis as an approach to decision-making (Chapter 7). For the moment it is enough to note that alternative theories and methods to understand and handle non-monetary change processes exist.

Efforts to counteract unsustainable trends:
Millennium Development Goals

As already indicated, sustainability is too often regarded as secondary in relation to economic growth and other indicators of market performance. There are some arenas where attempts to deal constructively with sustainability issues are made. Efforts to counteract unsustainable trends may take different forms from articulating what the problems are and raising consciousness and engagement to dialogue about appropriate policy and indicators for performance measurement. Although the potential role of each individual and each organization is a recurring theme in this book, I focus on efforts of a more official kind from the UN level via the EU down to my own country, region and municipality. The book is largely about conceptual and ideological frames of reference but institutional arrangements and administrative bodies are also covered to some extent. Even a case of planning, more precisely house construction in Uppsala municipality, will be discussed. Have the actors appearing in such a case 'internalized' the ideas of SD or do they continue as before (or is the situation even worse than it was some years ago)? The story told is fragmentary and incomplete, perhaps even unfair in relation to what a more far-reaching study might reveal, but the pieces of information presented are nevertheless believed to be relevant.

At the interstate level, the UN has been involved in various sustainability issues over the years. The MDGs exemplify recent efforts (United Nations, 2007). Eight groups of development goals have been articulated. The goals were formulated in the United Nations Millennium Declaration adopted by 189 nations in 2000. Most of the goals and targets were set to be achieved by the year 2015, with 1990 as the baseline. The following development goals are stressed:

1 Eradicate extreme poverty and hunger.
2 Achieve universal primary education.
3 Promote gender equality and empower women.
4 Reduce child mortality.
5 Improve maternal health.
6 Combat HIV/AIDS, malaria and other diseases.
7 Ensure environmental sustainability.
8 Develop a global partnership for development.

Together, the eight sets of goals form a holistic and multidimensional idea of development. Poverty, health, gender issues, urbanization and environment have often been treated as separate domains in UN conferences and other arenas. Here, they are combined to generate a total picture. Goals are generally expressed quantitatively, the idea being to approach a more sustainable world in a step-by-step fashion. Targets are formulated for specific regions and at an aggregate level for all regions and each aspect of development.

With few exceptions, the idea of 'development' reflected in the indicators is non-monetary in kind and the influence of neoclassical dogma about economic growth as the number one consideration is reduced. Non-monetary indicators about health, education, environment, etc. are often expressed as states or positions for specific points in time in accordance with the recommendations made earlier (see Table 2.1).

Although the quality of statistical information is less than perfect in many countries and some estimates rather shaky, the efforts made should be encouraged. Reading the interim report from 2007 conveys an overwhelming picture of what remains to be done (United Nations, 2007). One billion people live in urban slums (see also Davis, 2006). Eleven million children per year – 30,000 each day – die from preventable and treatable diseases. In sub-Saharan Africa, less than two-thirds of children are enrolled in primary school. Deaths connected with HIV/AIDS, malaria and tuberculosis still represent gigantic problems. In relation to expectations of climate change, progress is limited. We all need to learn about and contemplate facts and figures of this kind.

There are still some shortcomings in the statistics presented. No information is given for instance about people dying or otherwise suffering from the use of pesticides in agriculture. Depending on one's ideological orientation and list of priorities, it is always possible to argue that some aspects of development, such as those related to the environment, deserve special attention. The publication *Global Environmental Outlook, GEO 4. Environment for Development* (UNEP, 2007) is a related attempt to comprehensively assess progress towards SD and remaining problems. At an early stage in this 500-page report (pp10–11) it is argued that the environment is presented as just one of the MDGs and that the crucial role played by the environment (ecosystem services etc.) for all other millennium goals is not made sufficiently clear.

The GEO 4 report is subdivided into categories of environmental issues (atmosphere, land, water, biodiversity) that are displayed regionally. Issues of reversibility/irreversibility of impacts are discussed (UNEP, 2007), a theme that is further discussed in this book. The GEO 4 study uses the so-called DPSIR (drivers–pressures–states–impacts–responses) conceptual framework. Key drivers include demographics, production and consumption patterns, but in relation to the present book, it is of interest to note that ideology (for instance neo-liberalism) and paradigm in economics (for example neoclassical economics) are not included among the 'drivers'. Actually, when reading the GEO 4 report, one understands that many authors have been involved and that they sometimes differ with respect to theoretical perspective and ideological orientation. At one place it is argued that environmental degradation 'raises deep ethical questions that go beyond economic cost–benefit analysis' and that 'the question of justice is perhaps the greatest moral question emerging in relation to environmental change and sustainable development' (UNEP, 2007, pp10–11). At other places (p30 and p32) the report is back to optimal solutions in terms of CBA:

> [N]atural resources can be seen as a capital asset belonging to a general portfolio, which is comprised of other assets and capitals, including material, financial, human and social. Managing this portfolio in a good and sustainable manner to maximize its returns and benefits over time is good investment. It is also central to sustainable development.

The argument continues by discussing 'valuation' in the sense of 'monetary valuation' and 'different valuation approaches' (UNEP, 2007, p32). One approach is about 'determining the total value of the current flow of benefits from an ecosystem' another about 'determining the net benefits of an intervention that alters ecosystem conditions' with the purpose of assessing 'whether the intervention is worthwhile'.

In my judgement, one has to make a choice between the attempts to estimate total monetary value and attempts to clarify ethical issues in a broader sense. As will be made clear later on in this book, the continued recommendation to use CBA (as a part of neoclassical economics) can even be seen as an important part of the social and environmental problems faced. Although the GEO 4 is sometimes contradictory, describing development in a comprehensive way is a big step forward when compared to neoclassical ideas or ideas of progress limited to a single dimension. We can continue to study specific issues, such as urban slums, urbanization more generally (UN Habitat) or water management (Stockholm Water Week and Stockholm Water Symposium) but we also need to relate the different issues to each other. Specialization may have its advantages but to remain relevant, the study in specific fields has always to be integrated into broader ideas of development.

Efforts to counteract unsustainable trends: Environmental policy of the European Union

MDGs are as relevant to the EU as to other regions. Activities in different regions and countries affect each other. It is no longer possible to limit sustainability policy to one's own region or country. The climate change and ozone layer issues are examples of this and one can go on to discuss various health issues and biodiversity. In some areas such as climate change, the EU is among the main culprits. All countries are part of the same journey and no one can claim innocence in relation to future global developments. Past 'success', in terms of rates of economic growth, may turn out to be a relevant explanation for parts of the local and global environmental degradation observed. Europe, with its industries and trade relationships, also has a role – with connected responsibilities – in counteracting negative and supporting positive sustainability patterns in other parts of the world.

In the sixth environment action programme of the European Community (Commission of the European Communities, 2001a) a broad approach, not very different from the MDGs, is used. Unsustainable trends and their possible impacts are identified in Table 2.2. Eco-toxicology and connected threats to human health are stressed, so is pressure on vital natural resources. Similar ideas about the most important problems are reflected in the EU strategy for SD (Commission of the European Communities, 2001b).

Table 2.2 *Some unsustainable trends in the EU*

Unsustainable trends	Possible impacts
Climate change	Weather patterns, sea levels, etc.
Threats to public health	Persistent toxic substances, resistance to antibiotics, food safety risks
Pressure on vital natural resources	Biodiversity, fish stocks, fresh water, waste disposal
Poverty and social exclusion	Gap between rich and poor regions, vulnerable groups in run-down city areas
Transportation	Congestion and pollution

Source: Commission of the European Communities, 2001b, p5

The European Environment Agency has compiled information suggesting that a lot remains to be done also in our part of the world. Urban slums may be less of a problem in the EU but the consumption or exploitation of land connected with urbanization and transportation certainly has to be taken seriously. According to the European Environment Agency (2005, p17):

> *Recent analysis shows that more than 800,000 additional hectares of naturally productive land were converted into artificial surfaces for homes, offices, shops, factories, and roads, adding 6% to the continent's urban areas between 1990 and 2000. This is equivalent to three times the area of Luxembourg and represents a significant shrinking of natural capital.*

As is the case with the MDGs, the ideas of development inherent in EU environmental policy are primarily multidimensional and non-monetary in kind. Issues of positional thinking and irreversibility are observed to some extent although not yet sufficiently internalized into policy and praxis.

Efforts to counteract unsustainable trends: Environmental policy in Sweden and the municipality of Uppsala

In 1999, the Swedish Parliament adopted 15 national environmental quality objectives to be attained by the year 2020 (2050 in the case of the objective 'reduced climate impact'). In 2005, a 16th objective was added (Swedish Government, 2004/2005). The environmental objectives are:

1   reduced climate impact;
2   clean air;
3   natural acidification only;
4   a non-toxic environment;
5   a protective ozone layer;
6   a safe radiation environment;
7   zero eutrophication;
8   flourishing lakes and streams;
9   good quality groundwater;
10 a balanced marine environment;
11 thriving wetlands;
12 sustainable forests;
13 a varied agricultural landscape;
14 a magnificent mountain landscape;
15 a good built environment;
16 a rich diversity of plant and animal life.

For each environmental quality objective, relevant indicators have been chosen, as well as interim targets, usually for the year 2010. Performance is measured and evaluated. In a report (Naturvårdsverket, Miljövårdsrådet, 2007), it has been assessed that success is at best partial and that some environmental targets are more difficult to reach than others. Reduced climate change, a non-toxic environment, sustainable forests and zero eutrophication are said to be 'particularly difficult to reach'. Progress is reported for some targets such as those related to acidification (number 3 above), but the achievements largely refer to the period before 1999, when the environmental goals listed were formulated. Again, objectives have been formulated in non-monetary qualitative and quantitative terms. Issues of irreversible degradation of ecosystems and natural resources are at the heart of the analysis.

The 16 national environmental objectives are also used at the level of counties as a way of monitoring and assessing the result of development and environmental policy. They even appear at the level of municipalities. In my own municipality, the City of Uppsala, a number of planning instruments are used, such as a comprehensive plan covering the whole municipality (Uppsala kommun, 2005a). Connected to the comprehensive plan is a Strategic Environmental Assessment (Uppsala kommun, 2005b) and for Uppsala an Agenda 21 document *Points of Departure for a Good Environment and Sustainable Development* (Uppsala kommun, 1997) also exists. Uppsala has also adopted an environmental policy programme where a subset of the national environmental objectives is used (Uppsala kommun, 2006). There is even a specific climate strategy for Uppsala (Uppsala kommun, 2005c), and the potential contributions of R&D activities from Uppsala's two universities (Uppsala University and the Swedish University of Agricultural Sciences) are discussed.

Uppsala municipality is still small when compared with many cities in other countries. However, the population is growing fast, adding some 2000 persons each year. The political leadership of the city, until recently the Social Democrats together with the Green and the Left parties and now a right wing–liberal alliance, appears proud of this development. Uppsala is now the fourth largest Swedish city with about 180,000 inhabitants. It is argued that this growth has to be met with new housing facilities. In some cases, land that was previously used for industrial purposes is transformed into housing areas. In other cases, forests and agricultural land is exploited for new purposes. Uppsala's comprehensive plan makes the controversial suggestion that agricultural land close to existing urban surface can be used while agricultural land in other parts of the municipality should be protected.

A house construction project as example

In terms of planning instruments and rhetoric, Uppsala is not bad in relation to SD. In practice things do not turn out so well. Let us take a look at a special case of 'town planning'. Västra Nåntuna is one area where the political leadership has decided to implement a detailed development plan (see Figure 2.1). According to the plan, 10 hectares of agricultural land will be transformed to urban space. There are 140 dwellings planned in the form of villas and rented houses. I have myself questioned this project in the main local newspaper, *Upsala Nya Tidning*, but it can be argued that I am a biased person. On the other hand, each individual is guided by an ideological orientation and the test to be applied is rather whether that ideological orientation is compatible with specific interpretations of SD.

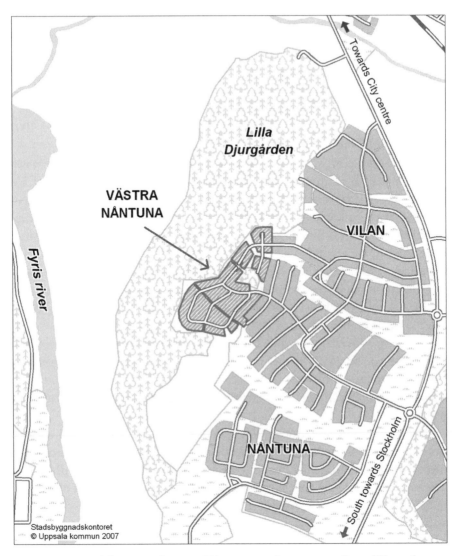

Figure 2.1 *The case of Västra Nåntuna in the municipality of Uppsala: Agricultural land is exploited for housing purposes*

Source: Lydia Haraldson/Peter Söderbaum

While there are legitimate interests to supply dwellings, other interests should also be considered. House construction on agricultural land is a form of land use discussed above as part of EU environmental policy. Lilla Djurgården (see Figure 2.1) is a recreational forest where people walk and run, mostly along a specific track. A buffer zone in relation to housing has existed in the form of a meadow to protect the recreational area and make it attractive. This meadow will be more or less eliminated if the plan is implemented. The area proposed for exploitation is close to areas rich in historical graves. Preliminary investigations by private parties suggest that there is also a cultural heritage worth protecting in the area. There are also other specific reasons to proceed cautiously. For example, Carl von Linnaeus, a world famous biologist, was a landowner in this area. He walked with his students on this land and 2007 commemorated the 300th anniversary of his birth.

At the time of writing, the Västra Nåntuna plan is subject to an administrative appeal. It is argued that an environmental impact assessment (EIA) should have been carried out according to Swedish Environmental Law (Miljöbalken), building law and EU directives, prior to the decision to accept the plan in the local building committee (Byggnadsnämnden). This was not done simply by arguing that 'no significant environmental impacts' were expected.[4] Another detail worth observing is that a specialist in environmental law was employed by the city until recently. When he made the judgement that an EIA should be carried out according to law, the leadership of the city reacted by recommending that he look for another job.

The city administration and JM AB, the construction company, act as if there were no problems. At the time of writing, construction work is going on concerning roads, houses for demonstration or marketing purposes and additional houses. This implies that environmental deterioration has started and will continue.

Those who live in existing villas bordering the area are worried about a troublesome traffic situation during construction and after completion of the project. Some will find their beautiful views of open land and forest disappear. The proposed and now partially implemented project exemplifies a number of the impacts that should – according to Swedish law – be carefully considered as part of an EIA:

- Nature encroachment of a largely irreversible kind: 10 hectares of meadows (agricultural land) is being transformed into urban space.
- Land-use changes of the present kind have implications for policies to mitigate climate change (carbon sequestration).
- Cultural heritage is affected. There are indications of cultural artefacts that should have been investigated. However, responsible persons at the county administration claim to know without investigation that there are no cultural artefacts and have approved the development plan.
- A popular recreational area (part of the Fyris River Reserve) is made less attractive by housing areas bordering the tracks for walking, running and horse-riding. It can be added that no study has been made about present utilization of the recreation area.

- Surface water from the new housing area will be led through the recreational area and may affect groundwater or the Fyris river (see Figure 2.1).
- Impacts upon biodiversity in terms of plant species, animals and birds have not been subject to study.
- Visual impacts for those living in previously existing houses have not been investigated.
- Noise and pollution during construction and after construction have not been investigated. Access roads to the new area go through existing housing areas and are not constructed to accommodate additional traffic.
- Existing infrastructure in terms of municipal heating systems will not be utilized in this case (existence of such infrastructure was part of the argument for the project).

Also, the number of persons negatively affected is large, a circumstance that should be considered according to environmental law. As I see it, the local politicians have largely avoided studying environmental and other impacts. To put it more bluntly the politicians have acted without knowing what they are doing. Instead they rely on cartels of promises between actors in the municipal administration, in the county administration and actors in the construction company. An EIA or some holistic approach to decision-making would probably have made a difference. In any case, I hope that some actors learn from this experience. The construction company is involved in even bigger projects in Uppsala so there are future opportunities to apply new learning and thinking.

For me, this is an extremely good illustration of the actual priorities in many political (and for that matter business) circles. The emphasis on economic growth and growth of cities suggests that 'sustainability' is understood in terms of 'business as usual', or 'ecological modernization', in this case. We shall not forget about all those who protest against this specific construction project. They may have interests as holders of private property or in enjoying walking in the forest but we can never deny them the right to have ideological opinions of a broader kind. In fact, some of those who protest may ideologically interpret sustainability in a way that is closer to the intentions of the UN, EU or Swedish official ideas of SD. The detailed development plan for Västra Nåntuna may even turn out to be incompatible with the Agenda 21 documents of Uppsala.

A lot remains to be done

There is a tendency for every political entity, such as Sweden as a nation or the Swedish Social Democrats as a political party or the present right–liberal alliance, to accept challenges such as SD and see them as a natural next step in aspiring for a better society. However, criticism of the previously dominating welfare concept tends to be downplayed. For the EU, the commitment to SD similarly adds to previous commitments. It can be seen as a minor change (c.f., 'ecological modernization') in relation to previous ideas about development or as a more radical change in ideological and political orientation (c.f, 'radical interpretation of SD'). As already indicated, the history of the EU from the Rome Treaty onwards is very much connected with neoclassical ideas of economic growth and the benefits from trade. The task was to prepare for the 'inner market' and improved competitiveness in relation to markets outside the EU. In addition, there are specific programmes to compensate or strengthen specific sectors and specific regions. The Common Agricultural Policy (CAP) and the different regional support programmes to reduce unemployment are examples of this.

For the smaller regions, such as Wales, Mälardalen or even Uppsala, one can guess that the idea of development has also been coined in market terms. The idea is to increase economic growth and employment at the regional level by improving competitiveness through innovation and entrepreneurship. Environmental protection has been taken seriously for some time but more as a correcting factor than as an essential part of a development concept. In recent years, a more multidimensional idea of development has emerged at the EU level as well as in specific countries or regions. Environmental and health issues have been strengthened in the agenda and 'environmental policy integration' is slowly gaining ground. The readiness to really change direction is an open issue and so many vested interests are connected with the traditional development path.

What would it mean to embark on a more radical idea of SD? To some extent, the answer has already been given. It would mean that non-degradation of the natural resource base and ethical commitments in relation to future generations in the home region and abroad are taken seriously. Each region would have an environmental and health 'foreign policy' in line with the radical SD concept. Democracy would be strengthened regionally through Local Agenda 21 and in other ways. Dominant ideas about theories of science, paradigms in economics, political ideologies and the present institutional framework would be challenged as part of a democratic and pluralistic strategy. We now turn to these issues.

Notes

1   There are signs, however, that at least the rhetoric is changing. At the UN Johannesburg conference in 1992, the Confederation of Swedish Enterprise presented a report arguing in favour of ecological modernization as the path for

Swedish industry to follow (Svenskt Näringsliv, 2002). It should be added that the author of this report is a consultant, Claes Sjöberg.

2　This principle essentially means that concerns about environment and natural resources should be part of all policy sectors and not be seen only as a separate sector.

3　It may be noted that Östros was recruited to become minister in the Swedish government directly from the (neoclassical) department of economics, Uppsala University.

4　Liv Hahne and Gunnar Hedberg, as presently acting municipal commissioners, (kommunalråd) are among those responsible. Hahne and Hedberg have made their attitude clear by supporting preparations for housing areas on agricultural land of 50 hectares and 150 hectares not far from the Västra Nåntuna area. It may appear strange to openly point to responsible politicians. This is, however, in accordance with the actor-oriented perspective of this study, normal imperatives of democracy and even the 'name and blame' environmental policy of the EU for cases where actors do not appear to take environmental issues seriously.

Further readings

For many actors, progress in society is very much connected with neoclassical ideas about economic growth and monetary profits. In his book *The Politics of Environmental Discourse. Ecological Modernization and the Policy Process* (1995), Hajer points to attempts in some circles to modify the present institutional framework to accommodate some of the worst environmental problems. But this is probably not enough and to prepare for more radical changes, one needs to listen to voices of civil society intellectuals, such as Vandana Shiva in her book *Earth Democracy* (2005) and David Korten in *When Corporations Rule the World* (2001).

Questions for discussion

➤ Why is SD a contested concept? What is your preferred interpretation of this concept?

➤ Do you agree with the assertion that a distinction between nonmonetary and monetary impacts (or indicators) and between flows and positions is essential for analysis of performance in relation to SD?

➤ In Chapter 2, SD has been discussed from the global to the local level. Emphasis has been on experiences from Uppsala. The idea is simply that each individual, wherever he or she lives, may identify cases of successful or questionable attempts to deal with climate change and other challenges. What are your experiences with your specific background? Are issues of irreversibility in non-monetary terms concerning environmental impacts observed and taken seriously in your neighbourhood, for example?

3

Sustainability Politics:
Are there Protected Zones in the
Development Dialogue?

Problems related to environment and development are formulated and under-stood in specific ways in policy documents used at the UN, EU, national and local levels. For example, EU documents, such as the previously mentioned staff working paper on the EU Strategy for Sustainable Development, the 6th environmental action programme or reports from the European Environment Agency are all very useful and relevant, and represent steps towards SD. However, it is still meaningful to critically discuss their content. There appear to be important social limits to the roles of those who write these documents. Patterns emerge that include certain lists of problems while forgetting about or perhaps deliberately excluding other ways of formulating problems at a more fundamental level. Are there 'prohibited zones' in the development dialogue?

Protected zones in the development dialogue – overview

The usual way of formulating environmental problems in the above-mentioned documents is to point to specific problems 'out in the fields' that may affect ecosystems and human health. Some problems relate to the atmosphere (climate change, ozone layer), others to ecosystems, natural resources (pollution with persistent chemicals, soil degradation, biological diversity, depletion of fish stocks, etc.) or health (food security, drinking water quality, air quality, noise, etc.). Problems can also be formulated in relation to specific geographical areas such as coastal zones, mountainous areas or marine zones. According to a third line of reasoning, environmental problems observed 'out in the fields' are discussed for specific societal sectors, such as agriculture, industry, transportation and energy, and it is argued that environmental issues have to be 'integrated' into agricultural policy, industrial policy, transportation policy and so on – indeed all kinds of policy.[1] Reference is made to the principle of environmental policy integration (EPI) (Lenschow, 2002).

This is fine. However, if one really wishes to make agriculture or industry or transportation compatible with SD, a more comprehensive problem formulation is needed. In the attempt to identify factors at a more fundamental level, I suggest that one should focus on the role of individuals and organizations as actors and the perspectives or worldviews of these actors. The beginning of an actor–network approach can be indicated by reference to three concepts: actors, agendas and arenas.

It is argued that 'actors' in different roles are at the heart of environmental problems, that actors are guided by their ideological orientation or 'agenda' and that they appear in different 'arenas' connected with their different roles and relationships. This actor perspective will be further developed in Chapters 4 and 6. Already at this stage it should be emphasized, however, that actors are related to social, institutional, physical and other contexts and that capability to act is constrained by this context. Decisions are made and behaviour may change but there are limits to options in terms of an actor's position in relation to various contexts as well as available information or knowledge. Reference can be made to 'path-dependence', implying that habits of thought and habitual behaviour play an important role.

An actor's ideological orientation (as well as her context) can also be described with respect to the following aspects:

- democracy;
- theory of science;
- paradigm;
- ideology;
- institutional arrangements;
- technology;
- lifestyle.

Actors may have different ideas about 'democracy' in society generally and in relation to specific spheres of activity, about the role of science in society (for example theories of science), about 'paradigms' in different disciplines or at an interdisciplinary level (for example the disciplinary paradigm of neoclassical economics), about useful means–ends philosophies in furthering progress in society, that is 'ideology' (for example GDP-growth ideology, neo-liberalism or some kind of green ideology), about the role of 'institutions' (for example the appropriateness of the present institutional framework for SD), about 'technology' (for example energy systems presently in use), and finally about desirable or appropriate 'lifestyles'. It is argued that the 'practice' or practical behaviour of actors in their different private, professional and other roles is very much related to the factors listed.

Many of these factors are of course considered in one way or another in the documents from the European Commission, the Swedish government or, for that matter, more limited regional entities. Technology is part of any analysis of energy systems and related CO_2 emissions. Lifestyle is, to some extent, discussed in terms of 'production and consumption patterns', although the criticism of our present lifestyles is quite restrained among 'establishment actors'. Minor institutional changes connected with new laws or directives are certainly discussed, while more fundamental changes are outside the scope of the agenda of EU policy-makers. There is nothing unexpected in this. The European Community, or EU, has a specific history and reflects a specific pattern of ideological development. At issue is now whether SD means anything new and opens the door for arguments and practices that have been played down in the past.

In every social setting, there are limits to what one can say or write. Many are those who have contributed to the dialogue about the EU and the previous European Community, actors from universities included. Like other actors, scholars from the universities too often behave in an opportunistic manner avoiding the big issues with the hope of being invited back to the table in the future. It seems extremely important that representatives of the universities do not forget about their independent and critical role in relation to society at large. Just as there should be a critical dialogue within universities and the scientific community, we should participate in a constructive dialogue in arenas outside universities.

Among the factors listed, it is argued here that very little of the development dialogue in the EU or in specific countries, such as Sweden, has been formulated in terms of the role of science in society, specific disciplinary paradigms and established or more recent ideological orientations (Söderbaum, 2004a). Concerning the role of science, it is generally assumed that science can only have a positive impact on society at large. I will argue that science certainly can have such a positive role but that science may also be part of the societal problems. As already indicated, economics is not a discipline without problems. Economics has been part of the mental map of the promoters of the European Community from the Rome Treaty onwards. The idea that the 'close to monopoly' position of neoclassical economics at university departments of economics in the EU can be a threat seems to be far away for most EU politicians and public servants. A vocabulary in terms of 'ideology' is part of the dialogue between EU politicians but seems to be largely neglected in EU official documents. It is assumed that ideology belongs to the sphere of politics and politicians. Civil servants can somehow write about 'policy' without referring to 'ideology', while politicians address issues of ideology more openly as part of a normal cooperation and competition in terms of political ideas. Scientists who claim to deal with problems in the EU in a holistic manner similarly too often feel that they are more 'scientific' if they refrain from a vocabulary in terms of 'ideology'. But if we are facing fundamental ideological issues, these aspects of the problems should also somehow be articulated and dealt with.

A debate about the role of science, about neoclassical economics and about how established ideologies relate to SD as an emerging ideological orientation may open the doors for some necessary new thinking, for institutional change processes, and hopefully new patterns of production and consumption. My background as an economist makes me focus on the role of economics and the need for pluralism in this discipline.

Criticism of science is largely avoided

Many understand science exclusively in positivist terms. Science is about seeking the 'truth', and the principles of objectivity and value neutrality are at the heart of this endeavour. Positivist science is about testing hypotheses with the intent to reveal regularities and, if possible, new scientific laws. Only one theoretical perspective is valid at a time for each field of study. Under exceptional circumstances, a 'paradigm shift' (Kuhn, 1970) may occur. This implies that a new paradigm replaces the old one. This model of good science is connected with natural sciences, including physics and chemistry. Scholars in the social sciences with a positivist orientation try to get as close to (their understanding of) the principles of natural science as possible.

This traditional idea (see the left-hand side of Table 3.1) of good science has not gone unchallenged. Evolutionary perspectives (right-hand side of Table 3.1), different from the mechanistic ideas of physical sciences, are gaining ground. There is a growing interest in describing and understanding patterns of change over time as opposed to focusing on movements from one state of equilibrium to another (right-hand side of Table 3.1). Scholars representing the social sciences have insisted on the importance of values in social science research (Myrdal, 1978) and any research that claims relevance in relation to societal objectives. Economics as a social science is not only science but also ideology as has been made clear in this study. Social and humanistic disciplines point to the importance of subjectivity in understanding human behaviour and to the role of different actors in the SD dialogue. Hermeneutics (Ricoeur, 1981), social constructivism (Berger and Luckmann, 1966), narrative analysis (Porter Abbot, 2002), discourse analysis (Howarth, 2000) and contextualism (Toulmin, 1990) are some catchphrases that are part of this new development. Our focus on the rhetoric and behaviour of actors makes interviews and conversation with individuals as actors in different roles an essential part of the research process.

Instead of (or in addition to) hypothesis testing and the search for regularities relevant for a larger population of individuals, organizations, ecosystems, etc., the interest to study and learn from individual cases is increasing in many disciplines, including business studies (for example, 'contextualism' to the right in Table 3.1). There may be both similarities and differences when comparing business corporations. The scholar can learn as much, if not more, from the differences by thinking in terms of unique companies operating in unique contexts. Instead of reductionism, for instance 'monetary reductionism', the study of impacts in multidimensional and holistic terms is regarded as fruitful. Causation can be perceived in multidirectional terms, as in the case of systems thinking and analysis, and the models used need not be limited to simplistic mathematics. Rather than looking for 'optimality' in a complex decision situation, the idea of 'illuminating' an issue may be more meaningful. Maximizing an objective function in search for optimality is appropriate only in the simple cases where relevant actors and stakeholders all agree about one specific objective function to be applied. In other cases, decision-makers or interested parties differ with respect to ideological orientation. This has to be reflected in the methods used to support dialogue and preference formation.

Table 3.1 *Epistemological tensions in studies for SD*

Traditional premises	Complementary (or alternative) premises
Mechanistic	Evolutionary
Value neutrality	Values unavoidable
Objectivity	Subjectivity (interpretative)
Universal regularities	Contextualism, uniqueness, case studies
Reductionism	Holism
One-directional causation	Multidirectional causation
Logically closed mathematical models	Pattern models that may be fragmentary
Optimal solutions	Illuminate, consensus seeking
Disseminate knowledge	Interactive learning, dialogue

Source: Norgaard, 1994, p62; Söderbaum, 2000, p26

For the social sciences, the idea of only one correct paradigm has to be abandoned. The presence of values and ideology in social science research suggests that a complementary relationship between theoretical perspectives or paradigms, each reflecting a specific ideological viewpoint, is relevant. Considering the unavoidable presence of values and that principles of democracy are applicable also for social science research, it is suggested that the idea of 'paradigm coexistence' (Söderbaum, 2000, pp29–31) is more constructive than that of 'paradigm-shift'.[2] Instead of being expert (in the extreme sense of the word), the social scientist becomes a more humble person who may act as facilitator in the search for ways and means to handle issues related to the environment and development.

As an example of the ideological content of specific models or theories we can point to 'economic man' as a model of the individual in neoclassical micro-economics and compare him with 'political economic person' (PEP) as an alternative model.[3] The neoclassical economic man (NEM) model is based on specific assumptions about human beings that are both scientific in a traditional sense and ideological and political. The individual is interpreted in relation to her market relationships (consumer, wage-earner, investor) while disregarding or downplaying all other roles and relationships (as citizen, professional, parent, etc.). According to PEP assumptions, the individual is understood holistically in scientific as well as ideological terms, including market as well as non-market roles. While the NEM is maximizing utility by buying alternative baskets of commodities, considering her monetary budget constraint with little or no consideration of the interest of others, our PEP is guided by an ideological orientation in all her roles and relationships. The PEP's ideological orientation may be narrow or broad in scope. Decisions in all spheres of human activity are understood in terms of matching ideological orientation with the expected impact profile (in multidimensional terms) of each alternative considered. In neoclassical theory, an individual's preferences and way of maximizing utility are given, i.e. accepted and not questioned. A scholar referring to the PEP model, by contrast, may be very interested in the ideological orientations of specific individuals and how they change. As an example, one person's values and ethics may be closer to a specific interpretation of SD than another's.

It goes without saying that if a scholar is interested in SD, it becomes relevant to focus on how individuals as actors interpret the world in ideological terms. This would include the person's roles as professional, citizen and consumer. How do people's stated values and ideological orientations relate to their actions in professional and other roles? Is there a discrepancy between rhetoric and practice? Distinguishing between differences in individuals' lifestyles becomes very relevant.

Now, in what sense would more emphasis on the right-hand side of Table 3.1 improve the prospects for a constructive approach to SD? My answer is that in a situation where a new direction for development is considered, we need to look beyond 'the field' and get closer to individuals as actors. At this level we can study individuals with respect to their worldviews (ideological orientation, ideas about economics, etc.). Actors in different roles are sometimes part of a solution and sometimes part of the problem. Actor studies become one of the many paths to follow. Examples of such studies are given in Chapter 6.

Another important recommendation is about the 'principle of pluralism' (Söderbaum, 1999, 2004b). We all believe more in some theoretical and ideological perspectives than others but we should be ready to listen and learn from advocates of competing perspectives. More than one perspective is often needed and one perspective is perhaps best understood by being compared and assessed relative to another.

Criticism of the monopoly of neoclassical economics is largely avoided

While there is a need to discuss theory of science in relation to SD, there are also reasons to focus on specific paradigms. It is argued here that very few politicians and civil servants have entered into a serious debate about the fruitfulness of neoclassical economics as a mental map to address the problems now faced.[4] The tendency is to assume that paradigm issues should be left to university scholars and have little to do with practical affairs. Mainstream neoclassical economics has become a 'protected zone' in the development dialogue carried out within the EU, the Organisation for Economic Co-operation and Development (OECD), the World Trade Organization (WTO) and many other arenas. The reasons behind this 'protectionism' are probably as much ideological as they are intellectual. Vested interests are involved and the debate about paradigms in economics is as much a power game involving competing ideological standpoints as it is a debate over 'good' science.

A majority of establishment actors still seem to believe that development and welfare can be reduced to economic growth in GDP terms and to monetary profits at the business level. SD becomes reduced to 'sustained growth' and 'sustained profits' in monetary terms. Surprisingly, the seriousness of present environmental and development problems has done little to raise questions about the monopoly of neoclassical economics. Instead, the tendency is to listen to neoclassical economists and their story about possible marginal failures. As already made clear, neoclassical economists connect environmental problems with the possibilities of 'market failure' and 'government failure'. Market transactions may influence third parties negatively and in these cases 'externalities should be internalized' and the PPP should be applied. Governments may subsidize activities that degrade natural resources and in these cases subsidies should be removed. This correction of failures is built on a neoclassical idea of 'correct' prices, as in CBA.

Proposals to internalize externalities or remove subsidies with harmful impacts on the environment are all worthy of consideration. The problem is rather that they are too seldom applied in practice. This may be explained by failures of a more fundamental kind in relation to some vision of a healthy development, such as those that have already been listed in the introductory part of this chapter. Most of these potential failures are outside the scope of neoclassical economics: theory of science failure, paradigm failure, ideology failure, institutional failure, failure of organizations as actors and failure of individuals as actors. Something may be wrong with the kind of paradigms, ideologies or institutional arrangements that have dominated for some time.

'Paradigm' here refers to 'conceptual and theoretical perspective' and neoclassical economics exemplifies a paradigm. Institutional theory is another paradigm with origins in economics and sociology. More recently, it has also been influential in economic history and organization theory. It is argued here that while neoclassical economics is useful for some purposes, it is not sufficient for all purposes. The close to monopoly position of neoclassical economics in university departments of economics around the world is a considerable problem. Pluralism is a necessity for reasons that will be explained below.

'Ideology' is used in a rather broad sense to refer to 'ideas about means and ends' or 'means–ends philosophy'. As previously indicated, ideology is about an actor's perception of present position in her context, perceptions of desired future positions and about how to get there. Therefore 'ideology' or 'ideological orientation' is not limited to established political ideologies, such as socialism, liberalism and various versions of 'ecologism' or 'green' ideology but is understood in much broader terms. It is assumed that an individual is guided by her 'ideological orientation', i.e. patterns of thought and values and that ideology therefore is not exclusively a collective phenomenon. Neoclassical economics, while being science in some sense, also qualifies as a 'means–ends philosophy', making it an ideology. In fact, neoclassical economics is more precise as an ideology than most of the established political ideologies mentioned. Neoclassical theory recommends and even imposes a view of human beings as consumers at the expense of all other roles (citizen, professional, parent, etc.), a view of organizations as firms or business companies at the expense of all other kinds of organization, and a specific view of markets in terms of supply and demand while other ideas of markets are not considered or play a negligible role. Neoclassical economics points to specific ideas of economics, efficiency, valuation, decision-making, social change and more. Together, these elements form both a kind of microeconomics and a very specific ideological orientation.

In Table 3.2, the neoclassical view is compared with an institutional perspective in some respects. As an alternative to NEM, a PEP is proposed. At the level of organizations, a political economic organization (PEO) is suggested as an alternative to the profit-maximizing firm. This is further elaborated in the pages to follow.

Terms such as 'consumerism', 'corporatism' and 'economism' suggest that some actors in society interpret neoclassical economics as highly ideological. Valuation is dealt with in monetary terms as part of the neoclassical efficiency concept. This implies that there is a kind of 'monetary reductionism'. When

Table 3.2 *A comparison between the neoclassical and an institutional conceptual framework*

View of:	Neoclassical economics	Institutional economics
History	Not very relevant	Evolutionary perspective, path-dependence
Individual	Economic man	PEP as actor
Organization	Profit-maximizing firm	PEO as actor
Economics	Ideologically closed idea of efficient resource allocation	Ideologically open ideas about efficiency and resource allocation
Decision-making	Optimization	Matching, appropriateness, pattern recognition
Approach to decision-making and sustainability assessment	CBA	Positional analysis (PA), EIA, etc.
Relationships between actors	Markets	Non-market and market
Market	Supply and demand for single commodities	Social (and power) relationship between market actors, fairness, multifunctionality, multiple commodities
Progress in society	Growth in GDP	Ideologically open – interpretations of SD among options

Source: Söderbaum, 2006, p185

neoclassical economists refer to 'correct' prices, they claim to be able to point out the 'best' or 'optimal' alternative for society from a perspective of resource allocation. Proponents of other ideologies are seldom as precise in their reasoning and conclusions. Institutional economics similarly concerns both science and ideology, and some of us who advocate this approach try to deal with this fact rather than deny it. It can, however, be argued that the relative open-endedness of institutional economics makes it less specific in ideological terms and thereby more compatible with democracy.

Neoclassical economics is connected with positivism as a theory of science. From this perspective, it is believed that objectivity and value neutrality are possible. As previously argued, the neoclassical project from 1870 onwards has been an attempt to make economics a 'pure' science. Economics is regarded as separate and separable from politics. According to this view, science and university education could not be part of the development problems faced. It is argued that university researchers study problems in a value-neutral way. They look for the 'truth' and nothing else. Nobody can blame them. Rather politicians and perhaps business actors are responsible. This view tends to dominate in spite of all that has happened in the theory of sciences in terms of an interest in the subjective and ideological aspects of human behaviour.

The need to replace neoclassical monopoly with pluralism can now be better understood. If each paradigm or scientific perspective is coloured by values and ideology, then the limitation to one paradigm at a university department is not compatible with normal ideas about democracy. Science and the universities should not back one particular ideology, such as the neoclassical 'market and economic growth' ideology, at the expense of other ideological options. Science should rather 'illuminate' an issue in relation to various possibly relevant ideological orientations. A well-known economist, Ezra Mishan, the author of a textbook on CBA (1971), has argued that the use of CBA for decision-making in society should be conditioned. There must be a consensus among citizens about the valuation rules built into CBA. According to Mishan, the polarized debate over environmental issues furthermore implies that consensus no longer exists (Mishan, 1980).[5] A Norwegian economist similarly identifies the ideology of CBA as being close to growth in GDP terms (Johansen, 1977). Such an ideological orientation is acceptable for some citizens or actors but not for others.

The case of neoclassical economics suggests that the mentioned failures (or factors indicated in the introduction to this chapter) cannot be seen in isolation. Paradigms are intertwined with ideology, and both are connected with institutions. Perhaps one should see development as influenced by a 'cluster' or 'package' of theory of science-paradigm-ideology-institutional arrangements. Neoclassical economics and neo-liberalism are compatible in many ways, the present growth-oriented market economy being the main institutional arrangement. Proponents of this 'cluster' systematically avoid many of the issues that have here been presented as fundamental. 'Market failure' and 'government failure' as recognized by neoclassical economists are only a subset of possible 'institutional failures'. As part of a broader view, the 'firm' or business corporation as an institution, while being celebrated as an 'engine of growth', may not be entirely well adapted to present needs. The size of business corporations is also an issue according to David Korten (2001) who questions the growth of trans-national companies in power terms and in relation to national governments, civil society and from the point of view of democracy. Still, the increased popularity of environmental management systems (EMSs) suggests that some institutional change processes that are positive (although limited) from an SD point of view are 'already' present in business circles.

Organizations other than business companies, for instance civil society organizations may also fail in some respects. They may – as much as many other establishment actors – avoid (or not understand the relevance of) an open discussion about paradigms in economics and ideology. Individuals may fail in professional and other roles and the total lifestyles of individuals can be problematic from an environmental, social and health-related point of view. Fortunately, there are also examples of 'success' and 'good practice' in the above respects.

Implicit in the previous arguments is that each specific interpretation of SD can be seen as an ideological orientation much like other ideological orientations. If the conceptual framework of neoclassical economics is more in line with 'business as usual' or at best, 'ecological modernization', this is not enough to guide us towards a radical vision of SD.

Criticism of the dominant economic growth ideology and neo-liberalism is largely avoided

For a long time, the many advocates of neo-liberalism dominated public debate. Margaret Thatcher became the UK's Prime Minister in 1979. She was referred to as the 'Iron Lady' and she saw herself as a disciple of Friedrich von Hayek. A belief in the beneficial aspects of markets became 'the major World religion with its dogmatic doctrine' (George, 2000 p29). One of the ideas is that markets can deal with or solve problems much better than governments, making privatization a step forward for a large number of activities. According to this view, even so-called 'natural monopolies', such as energy supply, water supply and railway services, are best managed by private business.[6] The Austrian school of economics, which included Friedrich von Hayek and later Milton Friedman, can be seen as an ideologically extreme version of a market-oriented theory.

For trans-national companies and business in general, neo-liberalism was an ideology that made life easier. Market expansion into every corner of the world, facilitated by the General Agreement on Tariffs and Trade (GATT) agreements and negotiations as part of the WTO, became a realistic option for many companies. It was argued that only a system where almost all kinds of resources were of the private property kind could be efficient. Neo-liberalism is a clear and simplistic ideology. Business companies should pursue their profit motives and individuals should work to get an income and be nice consumers. Some individuals will compete successfully with others and become important property owners and make capital investments according to monetary criteria.

Not everyone was happy with this ideology and connected practice (for example Self, 1993). The idea that public property cannot be managed efficiently was challenged and cases where local societies have developed rules to deal efficiently with 'common property resources' were described and discussed (for example Ostrom, 1990). More importantly, the 'efficiency' idea inherent in neoclassical and Austrian economics was questioned. Issues of justice or fairness were raised in relation to social and environmental problems. Stakeholders with only partially common interests but united in ideological terms as critics of neo-liberalism came together in social movements. As we all know, activists protested at Seattle, Washington DC, Gothenburg, etc. With the ambition of questioning the legitimacy of big businesses 'ruling the world', these actors also started to arrange their own meetings to discuss globalization and other issues (International Forum on Globalization, 2002).

Today, we are in a situation where a number of books have been published to interpret the various phenomena. Some point to the role of civil society and the activities of environmental organizations, such as Greenpeace, the World Wide Fund for Nature (WWF) or individual activists in different roles. Others discuss a new role and purpose for business (Cortright and Naughton, 2002) or refer to a civil corporation (Zadek, 2001) or corporate social responsibility (CSR) (Vogel, 2005). These authors also point to new partnerships where business can learn from civil society organizations. Zadek's (2001) book exemplifies a movement away from simplistic ideas about the role of business to a new role implying a degree of frustration and acceptance of complexity. Present unsustainable trends have to be counteracted even if this is a difficult task.

In Chapter 2, an attempt was made to define SD in broad terms. SD is multidimensional rather than one-dimensional; it raises issues of ethics in relation to future generations and to non-human life forms rather than avoids them; it involves a reference to the precautionary principle rather than an attitude of unreserved technological optimism and it relies on a number of principles of democracy as means to get closer to SD rather than a top-down expert-oriented approach. 'Ideology' has previously been defined as 'means–ends philosophy' and it appears clear that SD qualifies as an ideology or ideological orientation. If it means anything, SD stands for a new direction in societal development. 'Mental maps' that have been used to further progress along traditional lines have to be revisited and the possible usefulness of new mental maps can no longer be excluded.

Assuming now that SD stands for something different from the traditional theoretical perspectives touched upon – what are those differences? A first observation is that SD implies a commitment to work for a society in a way that does not systematically degrade the natural environment. This *value commitment* does not go well with positivism as a theory of science and its alleged value neutrality. As previously argued, SD is a multidimensional idea of development while neoclassical economics and the 'market and economic growth' ideology is one-dimensional in monetary terms. Similarly, ethical considerations are at the heart of SD while neoclassical economics relies exclusively on a specific kind of consequential ethics in utility or monetary terms. Egoism and even greediness are at the heart of this 'ethics'. While the precautionary principle is part of SD, this principle is seldom mentioned as part of neoclassical theory. The focus on democracy as a guide to public dialogue, decision-making and implementation does not have a recognizable counterpart in neoclassical theory. It can then be concluded that neither exclusive reliance on positivism, nor neoclassical economics go well with SD as here defined.

Another set of questions relates to conventional political ideologies: what about the main principles of neo-liberalism, social liberalism, socialism, social democracy, Christian democracy, ecologism – are they compatible with SD? Or to put it differently, how can neo-liberalism (social liberalism, socialism, social democracy, etc.) be changed to become more compatible with SD? Neo-liberalism with its simplistic ideas about markets solving all kinds of problems and support for privatization seems to be a perspective that, more than others, departs from SD.

At issue is whether and if so, how, can SD be 'integrated' into more traditional political ideologies. The ideology of green political parties is closer to SD but representatives of these groups should also take part in a debate about paradigms in economics, theory of science, etc.[7] I do, of course, not claim to have the final answer. I insist, however, on the importance of formulating questions of this kind. For politicians and other actors, traditional ideologies are of importance. These ideological orientations cannot be left unchanged in a situation where SD is supposed to gradually replace conventional development ideas.

Criticism of institutional arrangements is downplayed

Just as issues of theory of science, paradigms in specific disciplines and political ideologies are largely kept outside the development dialogue, so are the fundamental issues of institutional arrangements. The normal attitude is to assume that only marginal adjustments in present institutional arrangement are necessary or possible. Only few of us are ready to ask if 'capitalism' as an economic system is 'sustainable' (see O'Connor, 1994 for an exception) or compatible with 'sustainable development'. Even I hesitate to formulate problems in such terms. A first step might be to define 'capitalism' and discuss which economic systems qualify as 'capitalistic' according to a specific definition. In some sense, where 'state capitalism' is part of the concept, all possible economic systems are 'capitalistic'. In most cases, 'capitalism' refers to economic systems where most property is privately owned, where corporations play a major role, and where extension of this private sphere is believed to be desirable. It is clear that private property plays an important role in our present market economies and that the responsibilities connected with private property should be part of the SD dialogue. Smaller adjustments of the institutional framework can be observed all the time but the fact that minor institutional adjustments are accepted in most circles should not completely exclude the possibility of major changes.

SD is largely discussed at the societal level. However, it becomes difficult to imagine that SD at the macro level will be achieved if the behaviour of individuals and organizations at the micro level is not compatible with SD. Business corporations have always been regulated in some ways. Are these rules compatible with present needs? If, as an example, SD is understood in multidimensional terms, then one-dimensional measurement of goal achievement at the level of organizations, such as business companies, is not enough. We need EMSs to measure environmental performance and probably more than that. What will be the next step in terms of schemes of standardization or proactive business policy?

One starting point in our attempts to get closer to SD is, once more, the neoclassical paradigm. It seems important to open the door for interpretations of the individual in terms other than NEM and of the organization in terms other than profit-maximizing firms. There are similarly alternatives to an interpretation of markets in terms of supply and demand. A market can be interpreted in ways other than as an arena where greedy market actors meet to play their game and to carry out transactions. In some circles, a movement away from simplistic neoclassical ideas of markets seems to be occurring. If such changes continue, something may be gained. It should also be recognized that there are important non-market relationships at play as part of societal development. In the next chapter, I turn to these issues of understanding individuals and organizations as actors.

A non-reductionist idea of responsibility and accountability

Table 3.3 can be taken as a summary of this chapter and as a way of underlining the connectedness between ideas of science, paradigms in economics, ideology and the institutional framework. Positivism goes well with neoclassical economics and neo-liberalism to legitimize essential parts of the present institutional framework. This cluster of ideas is well protected but as we have seen can be challenged by other clusters of ideas, for instance those indicated in the right in Table 3.3. Rather than relying exclusively on positivism as a theory of science, additional theories of science are brought into the picture. 'Perspectivism' (Fay, 1996) as a label suggests that scientists or other scholars can learn a lot by considering different perspectives that may sometimes be complementary, sometimes competitive. At the level of paradigms, the version of institutional economics presented in this book is one possible perspective. A radical interpretation of SD is an ideological orientation that, together with other elements in the cluster, will hopefully contribute to a better world.

Table 3.3 *A way of illustrating tensions between worldviews*

	Predominant worldview	Alternative worldview
Theory of science	Positivism	Perspectivism
Paradigms in economics	Neoclassical	Institutional
Ideology	Neo-liberalism	Radical interpretation of sustainability
Institutions	Present institutional framework	Emerging alternative institutional framework

Table 3.3 suggests that comparison between paradigms in economics (for example neoclassical versus institutional economics) should not be seen in isolation. To understand the dominance of neoclassical economics in some circles, views about theory of science, the role of science in society and ideological preferences for and beliefs in specific institutional arrangements have to be brought into the picture.

Another way of summarizing the message of this chapter is to point to a number of simplifying assumptions or doctrines that have increasingly come into question. Examples of such simplifying assumptions, that now deserve serious reconsideration, are presented in the left in Table 3.4. Facing uncertainty and other aspects of complexity, the doctrines of specialization and separability, while still being important, have to make room for integration and holism and one gets a different set of assumptions or doctrines (right-hand side of the table).

Questioning simplistic ideas about specialization and separability should be seen as a change in emphasis rather than an exclusion of the former more simplistic statements. All actors have to make serious attempts to broaden their perspectives and make different kinds of impacts visible in analysis.

The story can be elaborated further. The assumption that one nation (municipality) for the purposes of analysis in relation to sustainability can easily be separated from other nations (municipalities) is challenged. Using climate change as the example, no single nation or city can solve the problems for its citizens by itself. Cooperation is necessary and various cooperative strategies have to be considered.

Table 3.4 *A possible interpretation of EPI is that a number of simplifying assumptions have to be abandoned or modified*

Simplifying assumptions	A more holistic and integrated view
Science can easily be separated from politics and politics from science	Science cannot be separated from politics and science has a role in politics. As an example, economics should correctly be named 'political economics'
Single sciences, such as economics, can be separated from other sciences and other sciences from economics	Economics cannot be seen in isolation from other social sciences. It is part of them and indeed of all sciences
Business can be separated from politics and politics from business	Business companies are political actors who may influence societal development individually and collectively through networks. For example, politicians can influence and put pressure on business actors to move closer to SD
Environment as one sector in the economy can be separated from other sectors and other sectors from environmental concerns	Concern for the environment is an integrated part of all sectors
Laws can easily be separated from other rules of behaviour and compliance with laws is all that matters	The importance of national laws and EU directives should not make us forget about other emerging and existing systems or rules such as those referred to as civil regulation or codes of conduct
One profession can be separated from other professions	Individuals that see themselves as belonging to one profession should also seek to develop their competence in relation to other professions and types of understanding to better comprehend their own role in society
The professional role of an individual can be separated from more private roles	All roles of an individual are related as parts of her or his identity
Production is easily separated from consumption	Actors in society often combine the two roles of being 'consumer' and 'producer'
One actor (i.e. market actor) or stakeholder is easily separated from other actors/stakeholders	An actor/stakeholder is normally part of various relationships, networks and organizations in society and as a result may consider the interests of various 'others' rather than focusing exclusively on self-interest
Actors in a business company can exclusively focus on one stakeholder category (shareholders) while downplaying all the others	All stakeholders related to a company have to be considered as well as the role of the company and business as a whole in society. There may be priorities between stakeholders that vary over time
Issues of governance in society can be limited to politicians, for instance at the national and local (municipal) levels	Governance in relation to SD has to involve national and local government as well as all the other actors and stakeholders that are part of the development process
Responsibility and accountability should be limited and simple	Extended responsibility and accountability for individuals and organizations as actors in relation to social and environmental issues is desirable
The economy and markets can be regarded as separate from natural resources and environmental services	The economy is embedded in the ecosphere and the former cannot be separated from the latter

Notes

1   It can be noted that among 'sectors', for instance 'university research and education' is never mentioned as a potential problem area in relation to SD.
2   As part of the idea of 'paradigm coexistence', there may still be a shift in 'dominant paradigm'.
3   PEP assumptions are further elaborated in Chapter 4.
4   There are of course exceptions to this general observation. A member of the Swedish Parliament and Social Democrat, Lena Klevenås, asked the Minister of Finance in an open interpellation about the possibility of a debate about economic policy on the basis of ecological economics rather than mainstream neoclassical economics. The assumption of NEM is not a good starting point for economic policy, she argued (The Riksdag, Interpellation 1996/97:168). Her question was taken seriously, at least in part, and representatives of three political parties participated in the debate that followed. Another exception is that of the German Ministry of Education and Research mentioned in Chapter 1.
5   It may be noted that Mishan is also the author of *The Costs of Economic Growth* (1967) and is one of the contributors to 'A Blueprint for Survival' (*The Ecologist*, 1972) presented at the time of the Stockholm Conference on the Human Environment 1972.
6   While also neoclassical economics is centred on this role of the market, it should be recognized that it rather warns against privatization in the case of natural monopolies.
7   A more systematic attempt to address these issues is made by the Green Economics Institute, UK, where economists, politicians and others exchange views at conferences and in the *IJGE*.

Further readings

While many actors understand that present sustainability challenges are complex and difficult to handle, the dialogue about sustainability policy is still largely based upon the assumption that problems can be handled within the scope of dominant ideas about science, economics and ideology. To introduce alternative ideas, we need again to listen to civil society intellectuals, for example the authors behind *Alternatives to Globalization. A Better World is Possible* (International Forum on Globalization, 2002). Eva Kras's book *The Blockage. Rethinking Organizational Principles for the 21st Century* (2007) is also relevant here.

Questions for discussion

➤ Do you think that positivism as a theory of science is sufficient or that there is a need for a more pluralistic attitude?

➤ One thesis in Chapter 3 is that the combination of neoclassical economics and neo-liberalism supports and in a sense explains

many of the institutions that now appear to be increasingly problematic in relation to sustainability. Any serious dialogue about
policy and politics for sustainability has therefore to open the door
for competing theoretical perspectives in economics and competing
ideological orientations. Do you agree with this diagnosis about the
role of neoclassical economics and neo-liberalism?

➤ Would you say that the monopoly position of neoclassical economics at university departments of economics is something to be left
to the neoclassical economists themselves to consider or is there a
role for outside intervention? If intervention from outside is judged
necessary, would you say that 'market-based instruments' or
'command and control' instruments should be used?

➤ Policy and politics in relation to sustainability and progress in
society is built on a number of simplifying assumptions (see Table
3.4) that now have to be challenged. Do you agree?

4

From Economic Man to Political Economic Person

If 'business as usual', in terms of paradigm, ideology and institutional arrangements, is not enough to guide us towards SD, then we need to consider ways of consciously modifying or changing our mental maps or conceptual frameworks. The idea is to present a conceptual framework that a variety of actors will find helpful when thinking about and developing the idea of SD. I will emphasize concepts at the micro level that together form the embryo of a new microeconomics. This microeconomics is both related to and opens the doors for new thinking at the macro level.

Assuming that a number of individuals would like to see a transformation of society in the direction of SD – what kind of conceptual understanding of human beings, business companies and other organizations will facilitate such transformation? Just as neoclassical economics in many ways represents a specific ideological orientation, our present effort can be described as an attempt to construct an economics more in line with the ideology of SD. Some readers may find this attempt a bit unusual and strange. They may even call it utopian in relation to how they understand the functioning of our present society. These individuals may have become accustomed to the thinking habits connected with neo-liberalism and neoclassical economics, with their limited liability or responsibility doctrines. If this is the case, I can fully understand such reactions. Thinking habits and, even more, ideological orientations are not easily changed. However, the fact that there is considerable inertia involved should not cause us to abstain from trying to gradually change a society and an economic system that exhibits signs of being unsustainable.

Ecological economics can be described as 'economics for sustainable development' or 'sustainability economics'. 'Economics in the spirit of Agenda 21' is a similar definition. There is a commitment to work for SD and, more precisely, for the more radical interpretation of SD. In doing this, a pluralistic and open-minded attitude to different theories of science and disciplines becomes a virtue. The idea is no longer one of defending one particular theory of science or discipline but rather to borrow useful elements from different disciplines. Pluralism does not mean that 'anything goes'. We all have our cognitive habits and preferences. In my case institutional theory plays an important role.

The conceptual framework proposed is deliberated from the straitjacket of the simple mathematics that characterizes neoclassical economics. Mathematics has a role in economics and other social sciences but only in the case that one is aware of the limitations of mathematics as a language. In the present study, the neoclassical ideal of a closed logical-mathematical framework is abandoned. In fact, the over-reliance on mathematics in neoclassical economics combined with the claim for monopoly or lack of pluralism appear to be two of the main reasons behind the current crisis at departments of economics in most Western universities. They also contribute to the lag behind other social sciences. In the present study, as in many social sciences, qualitative analysis is considered fundamental and the conceptual framework to be suggested is not reducible to simple equations.

Political economic person

The previous analysis suggests that the economic man of neoclassical analysis is not compatible with the worldview or mental map advocated here. The neoclassical worldview is clear in many ways. However, it is overly simplistic and runs contrary to the acceptance of some degree of complexity. As an example, NEM is exclusively related to a market context and the individual is essentially seen as a consumer maximizing utility, subject to a monetary budget constraint. While it is difficult to question a statement that people maximize utility in some sense, it is equally true that such a statement is rather empty and uninteresting in relation to present environmental and development issues. Our interest is rather to find out how individuals differ with respect to utility maximization, or in our language, ideological orientations and lifestyles. To what extent is the ideological orientation of a specific individual compatible with specific interpretations of SD? We are also interested in ways of influencing the ideological orientations of individuals to make them gradually become more compatible with SD.

As an alternative more in line with institutional theory and the theoretical framework of social psychology, the PEP is proposed,[1] i.e. an individual with many roles (professional, consumer, citizen, parent, etc.) and relationships who is referring to a specific 'cognitive map' or worldview and guided by a political or 'ideological orientation' (see Figure 4.1). The individual has an identity and is positioned in, and interacts with, a context that is social, institutional, physical (man-made) and ecological. This adaptation to a context that is more or less changing over time is essentially understood in terms of the individual's ideological orientation and behavioural habits. Both ideological orientation and behavioural habits may change or be modified over time as a result of interactive learning and decision-making.

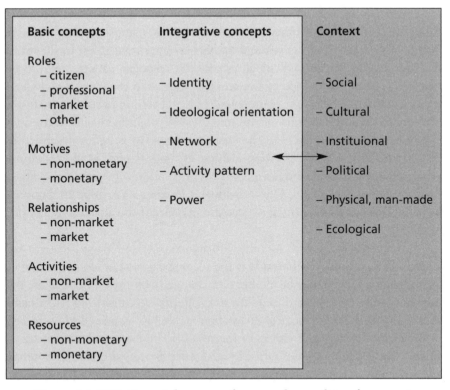

Figure 4.1 *PEP: Essential concepts for an understanding of a person's behaviour and adaptation to her or his context*

Source: Söderbaum, 2007a, p617

In Figure 4.1, a distinction is made between 'conceptual elements' or 'basic concepts' and 'integrative concepts'. Roles (and relationships) are part of a person's identity; motives and interests are elements as part of the individual's ideological orientation; specific relationships are part of networks; specific activities are part of the individual's total activity pattern or lifestyle; resources of different kinds are part of the individual's power position. As previously indicated, the individual is positioned in and moves in relation to a context. This context consists of other individuals and collectivities that can be described in social and cultural terms. The individual also relates to an institutional (non-market and market) context. From the point of view of the individual, this institutional context can be understood in terms of interpretations of various phenomena, including systems of behavioural rules. In addition, there is a physical and ecological context. The individual both influences her context (by choosing a specific path in geographical terms, for instance) and adapts to her context.

A person's adaptation to a changing context is largely habitual. Thinking habits are part of the individual's mental or cognitive map. Cognitive habits, or 'habits of thought', and behavioural habits play important roles. In situations that are familiar for the individual, established response patterns tend to be repeated. The individual sometimes sees few reasons to change either ideological orientation or behaviour with connected expected impacts. Alternatively, new situations and new information might cause the individual to reconsider established habits. In this case, the adaptation process is better described in decision-making terms. Decision-making is understood as a 'matching' process. The individual matches ideological orientation with each of the different alternatives considered. Our individual is looking for a 'good fit' between ideological orientation and the expected outcomes of the alternatives considered.

As suggested in Figure 4.2, this process can be understood in terms of 'pattern recognition'. On one side is the ideological orientation or pattern of the individual (which may be modified or changed), on the other hand are the pattern of impacts expected to follow each alternative considered (right-hand side of Figure 4.2). 'Ideological orientation' as well as 'expected impacts' can be understood in terms of visions or images of desired and undesired states of affairs. These visions are described in qualitative as well as quantitative terms and are, more or less, fragmentary, incomplete and uncertain in other respects. Objectives may be formulated in multidimensional, qualitative and/or quantitative terms; the same is true of expected impacts of alternatives related to such objectives.

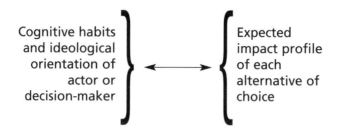

Figure 4.2 *Habitual behaviour and decision-making can be seen as a matter of matching ideological orientation and expected impacts*

One aspect of this way of approaching decision-making is that the concepts of 'rationality' and 'efficiency' are related to the individual's ideological orientation or to the ideological orientation in a group or other collectivity. Actor A, with a 'green' ideological orientation will perceive rationality and efficiency differently from Actor B, who may rely on a 'business as usual' ideology.

Neoclassical ideas about a common efficiency and rationality concept for all members of society are abandoned. As an example, conventional CBA can no longer be taken seriously as an approach to decision-making (c.f., Chapter 7).

Adapting to a changing context is mainly understood in terms of interactive learning processes that involve other individuals. Relating to a changing context is not always easy. The individual may experience tensions between different egoistic motives, different 'other-related' motives, etc. He or she may experience dissonance when facing conflicting messages from other individuals or actors. Information is perceived selectively and individuals use various 'defence mechanisms', such as the simplistic assumptions about various phenomena, exemplified in Table 3.4. Doctrines or cognitive habits about 'limited responsibility' and connected ways of 'externalizing responsibility' to others are certainly popular. However, the degree to which responsibility is externalized may vary in terms of the three types of ideological orientation: 'business as usual', 'social and ecological modernization' and a 'radical interpretation of SD'.

Whereas self-interest is a dominant feature of NEM assumptions, it is here assumed that a healthy individual has a strong ego but is able to at the same time more or less internalize the interests of others. In his book, *The Moral Dimension. Toward a New Economics*, Amitai Etzioni (1988) speaks of an 'I and we paradigm'. According to this view, each individual is part of a number of 'we-categories'. As a person, I may be concerned about my family as one 'we-category', colleagues at my workplace as another we-category, my home town, the people in my region, and, to some extent, the global society. PEP is a potentially responsible actor who, through networks and organizations, can influence development processes at various levels.

While there is some room for change, also inertia (Söderbaum, 1973) or 'path-dependence' (see for example North, 1990, 2005) are important characteristics of both the individual and her context. Inertia can be of many different kinds, such as the mentioned cognitive habits of influential actors or stakeholders, social commitments between individuals within networks or organizations (who may promise each other to act in specific ways), ethical and political commitments, established laws or other rules of conduct and contracts with suppliers or other cooperating partners. Thus, social change processes can be seen as a matter of actors moving around looking for open rather than closed doors. 'Vested interests' may make change difficult in many cases.

Why is this particular model of the individual chosen? At issue is whether or not an explanatory model is preferable to other models, or whether a model adds to the understanding offered by other models. In relation to this vantage point, it can be argued that PEP adds to the understanding offered by NEM and to the models of man from other social sciences.[2] While still relying on some simplifications, the PEP model is more complex and more realistic than the NEM model. In her book, Mary Clark (2002) questions the atomistic view of individuals in game theory and other parts of neoclassical economics. She suggests that human beings and other primates are best characterized by co-operative relationships and 'bonding'. As a professor of biology who has become engaged in theories of conflict resolution, she argues that NEM is not a good model of man from an explanatory point of view. Clark argues that this model can even be considered dangerous to our societies.

Social change in neoclassical economics is essentially understood as a result of changes in externally imposed incentive systems (for example environmental taxes or charges) while the individual's utility-maximizing function is essentially given. According to PEP assumptions, the ideological orientation or motives of an individual as actor may also change, suggesting that there are 'internal incentive systems' affecting behaviour, for example related to the individual's feelings of responsibility. Thus changes in behaviour may occur in a situation where external incentives systems are unchanged. It is the combined impact of external and internal incentives that may change behaviour.

However, since according to our previous arguments, each model necessarily is specific in ideological terms, a model may be preferred also for ideological reasons. From this point of view, it is believed that the PEP model is largely compatible with democracy as a meta-ideology and with our focus on getting closer to an SD path. More precisely, the PEP model is based on the belief that social change, in relation to environmental or development issues, begins with individuals who act by themselves and in cooperation with others. It is not enough to focus on environmental and other performance indicators of business organizations or society as a whole. In addition, individuals, as actors in different roles, should be made visible both when they behave in environmentally friendly ways and when they ignore environmental issues.

The present actor-oriented approach also points to the importance of empirical studies that focus on the cognitive habits and ideological orientation of individuals in specific roles in relation to a specific environmental or developmental issue. In addition to more conventional impact studies, conversation and dialogue with actors is viewed as a way forward (c.f., Chapter 6).

The present study is of a comparative kind and Table 4.1 is an attempt to summarize the previous discussion. NEM is systematically compared to PEP in a number of ways. History is an important part of the PEP model (with a focus on 'inertia' and 'path-dependence', for instance) but more or less neglected in mainstream neoclassical theory. The context of PEP is no longer limited to markets, as in the case of NEM. More roles than the market-related roles of consumer and wage earner are relevant. Interaction with others is not limited to markets and market actors are no longer exclusively selfish. They often cooperate with other actors considering their interests as well (Clark,

2002). Ideological orientation is proposed as a guiding principle rather than the utility maximization of NEM. Behaviour may be habitual and is not always a matter of conscious decision-making as in neoclassical theory. At an early stage, Thorstein Veblen and other institutional economists pointed to the role of habits in economic affairs. Today, this emphasis on 'rule-following' is also part of institutional organization theory, economic history, etc.

Table 4.1 *Two schemes of interpretation: NEM versus PEP*

Aspects compared	Neoclassical economic man	Political economic person
Historical dimension	Not considered relevant	The individual is a product of her history and relationships to specific contexts
Context	Markets for products and factors of production	Political, socio-cultural, institutional (for example market), physical (man-made), ecological
Roles	Consumer, wage-earner	Citizen, parent, professional, market-related roles, etc.
Relationships	Market relationships between selfish market actors	Market and non-market relationships of a cooperative or non-cooperative kind
Availability of information	Perfect information assumed	Search activities to reduce uncertainty about ideological orientation, alternatives and impacts
Values	Maximum utility of commodities within budget constraint	Ideological orientation as guiding principle, for example green orientation
Behaviour	Optimizing	Habitual, 'rule-following', also learning and conscious choice (decisions)

Source: Söderbaum, 2001 p187

From neoclassical theory of the firm to political economic organization

The only organization considered in neoclassical microeconomics is the profit-maximizing firm. In relation to the challenge of SD, other kinds of organizations are also of interest, such as civil society organizations (for example Greenpeace), universities and other public entities (see Table 4.2). Models of profit maximization remain relevant for business organizations although the challenge of CSR suggests that monetary calculation represents a partial, rather than total, basis for business decision-making (Vogel, 2005). While monetary considerations are important also for 'non-business organizations', the missions of such organizations are hardly limited to monetary profits (see Table 4.2).

Table 4.2 *Potentially relevant models/interpretations for business and non-business organizations*

Interpretation (model)	Business organization	Non-business organization
Profit maximization	X	–
Stakeholder	X	X
Network	X	X
Political economic organization	X	X

In the business management literature, alternative ways of interpreting business organizations have been available for some time. The stakeholder model is one early alternative to interpretations exclusively in terms of monetary profits (Freeman, 1984). Stakeholders are individuals who are concerned about or have something 'at stake' in relation to the activities of an organization or a specific decision situation. Pointing to different categories of stakeholders, including shareholders, customers, employees, board members, a chief executive officer (CEO) and people living in the neighbourhood, is a step forward in admitting that some conflicts of interest are normally involved in decision-making about operational activities or investment projects. As part of presenting the stakeholder model, there may still be a tendency to pack all shareholders together, all employees, etc. into homogeneous categories. This is a simplification; we know that individuals within a category (such as shareholders or employees) may have different interests and differ with respect to ideological orientation.

A second alternative to the neoclassical theory of the firm is the network model of organizations. According to this model or interpretation, the organization is essentially understood as an actor with relationships to other actors (Håkansson, 1982; Ford, 1990; Håkansson and Snehota, 1995). As in the neoclassical theory of the firm, market relationships are emphasized. While the focus is often on interaction between two market actors, the network idea points to connections (and interdependencies), including an extended set of market actors. Individuals connected with organizations are part of relationships and networks suggesting that social, psychological and even cultural aspects may characterize a relationship. Actors may or may not trust each other, and there may be proximity or distance in terms of geography, language, etc. One implication of the network approach is that the border between organizations becomes a bit blurred or ambiguous. Market actor A, while being part of one organization, may more or less be concerned about the impact upon other actors in the same network when facing decision situations or strategic options. Expressed in the previous language, actor A may regard other actors in a network as part of a 'we-category' (in terms of the I and we paradigm). It is also possible to refer to social and institutional 'embeddedness' of the actor or organization that facilitates some actions and becomes a barrier for other actions.

The actor (individual or organization) is embedded in various cooperative relationships and networks with other actors. Two organizations, as actors, may compete in relation to some activities (business companies engaged in technological development and market penetration) and cooperate in relation to others (lobbying activities in relation to regulatory entities, such as the Commission of the EU).

Network thinking also raises other issues: will the system that our organization belongs to be successful in relation to competing networks and systems? Are we happy with our network? Should we try to become part of some other existing network or build a new one in a step-by-step fashion? It is clear that the network model brings in social aspects and interdependencies of a kind largely absent in neoclassical theory. While this is a step forward, something is still missing in relation to the sustainability challenge emphasized in this book.

It should be made clear that the models or interpretations discussed should not be understood as a matter of 'either or'. Each model can contribute to our understanding. The neoclassical model, while being reductionist, tells us that there is a monetary aspect to be considered in most organizations. The stakeholder model suggests that it is not realistic to assume that all individuals and organizations related to an organization agree about a common objective function. It is normal for some conflicts of interest to exist, implying that there is a role for dialogue and negotiations. The network model adds a social dimension to this complexity. For example, it assumes that stakeholders or actors are not independent but related to each other in terms of confidence, trust, goodwill, etc.

As a complementary model, the PEO is proposed. Five additional features are stressed:

1 The organization as actor is interpreted in political terms. Issues of power, ethics and ideology are involved within the organization and in relation to various elements in its context.
2 Each individual connected with the organization is interpreted as a PEP with a specific ideological orientation. In this sense, the organization is assumed to be 'polycentric'. There is still normally some degree of commonality with respect to interests among individuals related to the organization.

3 Elements of hierarchy exist in every organization but the visibility of the individual as part of a PEO suggests a less hierarchic, more open and democratic organization.

4 The mission of an organization is understood in multidimensional and multifunctional terms, where the monetary dimension is only a part. Organizational performance is also measured and considered in multidimensional, multifunctional and ethical terms.

5 Conflicts and tensions between individuals and stakeholders are regarded as normal and partly constructive for the successful performance of the organization.

Choosing among interpretations of SD is not neutral in political terms. Issues of ethics and ideology are brought into the picture and for the same reasons that individuals are regarded as PEPs, organizations are interpreted in these terms. Business organizations as well as non-business organizations are actors referred to as PEOs. Organizations may, to some extent, internalize sustainability issues into their mission statements or refer to a 'business as usual' strategy. As actors in a democratic society, organizations may either bring us further away from or closer towards an SD path.

While the organization is a collective actor, it is at the same time composed of individuals as actors, each with a particular ideological orientation. A PEO is then composed of a number of PEPs, implying that the organization is regarded as 'polycentric' where each individual represents particular roles, relationships and an ideological orientation. In the case of a business company or other organization that steps in a green direction by becoming ISO 14001 certified, some individuals normally take the lead and become 'environmental entrepreneurs' while others are followers. Assuming heterogeneity, i.e. relying on the 'heterogeneity principle' in each actor category, such as those working for a company, seems once more to be a fruitful strategy in the study of social and institutional change processes (see Chapter 6).

CSR is a growing and frequently discussed topic. Although interpretations may differ, this discourse points to another feature of the PEO model. The performance of an organization is understood in multidimensional terms as opposed to the monetary reductionism of the neoclassical theory of the firm. The impacts following from a firm's actions can also be understood and described in functional terms in relation to various social and ecological systems affected.

The relevance of different organizational models has here been discussed mainly in relation to business organizations. It is argued, however, that the models, with the exception of the neoclassical theory of the firm, are equally relevant for non-business organizations (see Table 4.2). A university, for instance, can be understood in terms of its stakeholders, in network terms or as a PEO.

Table 4.3 brings us back to our ambition to compare neoclassical and institutional theory. It also summarizes the features of an interpretation in terms of PEO. Only some of the differences indicated will be discussed further.

Table 4.3 *Organizations: The neoclassical and an institutional view*

Aspects compared	Profit-maximizing firm	Political economic organization
Historical dimension	Not considered relevant	The organization is a product of its history
Context	Markets for products and factors of production	Political, socio-cultural, institutional (for example market), physical (man-made), ecological
Justification for existence	Profits for shareholders	Business concept, mission statement, 'core values', political ideology, social responsibility
View of individual	The organization is hierarchical making the individual largely invisible	Polycentric organization with individuals, PEPs, guided by their ideological orientation
Relationships	Internally: largely invisible, Externally: market relationships	Interaction (cooperative and non-cooperative) between individuals as actors, internally and externally, market and non-market
Availability of information	Perfect information assumed	Search activities to reduce uncertainty about ideological orientation, alternatives and impacts
Interests related to organization	Consensus idea based on assumed shareholder values	A complex of common and conflicting interests between stakeholder categories and individuals as actors
Decision act	Optimizing; maximum profits	Multidimensional impact studies, also rule following; matching ideology with expected impacts

Neoclassical economics and neo-liberal ideology have played an important role in the development dialogue and tend to see business corporations as the only kind of organizations. The terminology of PEO differs by also referring to organizations other than 'firms' (business companies) that influence 'economic development' in a broad sense. Universities or churches exemplify potentially influential organizations. The existence of some heterogeneity among individuals in each organization is compatible with a degree of commonality and consensus about the ideological orientation of the organization. In business, for instance, reference is sometimes made to 'core values' that should be observed in policy-making and operational activities.[3]

Democracy for problem-solving, security and sustainability

Behind our emphasis on the political aspect and the argument that economics is always political economics is a belief in democracy as a system of governance. Sometimes one hears doubts about democracy. For example, some scientists argue that environmental degradation has gone too far and that central powers must be strengthened and experts called in to find solutions to the sustainability challenge.

There is certainly a need for expert knowledge and also perhaps to strengthen central powers at the national or global levels. However, relying on experts may also be a dangerous strategy. Over-reliance on experts is sometimes referred to as 'technocracy' or 'econocracy' (Self, 1975) (i.e. a situation where scientists are assumed to know the 'correct' solutions and politicians are no longer needed). The first priority, as I see it, is to strengthen democracy. While some communities and countries are doing well in terms of democracy, there are opportunities for further improvements in most of them.

Getting closer to SD is not only about finding technical solutions to well-defined problems. It is also a matter of visions and ideology where citizens and politicians have a specific role. As many individuals as possible should participate in a dialogue about the future. Only when a large segment of the population, whether in a municipality or country, is committed to take sustainability issues seriously will action at different levels follow. The actions can extend from the lifestyles of individuals through organizations and local communities into the national and, eventually, global community.

Articulating visions, ideologies and problems to be solved must be done in many kinds of arenas with many different actors involved. Technocrats, who assume that theory of science, theoretical perspectives in economics, predominant ideologies and predominant lifestyles cannot be changed, can be considered part of the problems faced.

With increasing specialization, the subject of democracy itself has become an area of expertise. It is generally explored by students of political science or governance. Robert A. Dahl and Charles E. Lindblom belong to the forerunners (Dahl and Lindblom, 1953; Lindblom, 1977; Dahl, 1989) but many others have followed (for example Holden, 2000; Florini, 2003; Shiva, 2005; Held, 2006). Fortunately, democracy is a field of multifaceted research implying that there are many schools of thought rather than monopoly for one coherent set of ideas. Recent arguments for 'deliberative democracy' stand for the idea of bringing in as many persons as possible in a dialogue and interactive learning process. Learning is not only a matter of cause–end relationships but also deliberations about visions and ideology. Do we agree on sustainability as a vision? Do we have similar ideas about what it means? Is action to limit climate change among the first priorities or just one among many considerations?

Democracy also functions as a system of social control. Arenas where debate takes place and decisions are made should be open forums rather than closed; transparency should be a key consideration. Politically elected persons are responsible and accountable for their actions and decisions. This must also be true for other actors. Citizens and actors in other roles that watch what goes on in society are part of a security system that differs in kind from that of an organization or country led by a dictator. In relation to SD, environmental activists and organizations that challenge actions and trends perceived as unsustainable are very much needed. Just as a critical attitude can be constructive in science, the same is true of public debate. Accepting the existence of more than one ideological orientation appears to be an essential characteristic of democracy.

Notes

1   PEP and other parts of this alternative microeconomics is outlined in Söderbaum (1999, 2000) and is discussed for instance by Jakubowski (1999, 2000). A concept that is close to PEP, 'homo politicus', has been suggested by Faber et al (2002). Reference to homo politicus may be made also at departments of political science (or governance) but the tendency appears to be to discuss politics and ideologies at a collective level, for example for political parties.

2   Political scientists similarly point to 'citizenship' when arguing for a strengthened democracy and more active role for individuals in relation to environmental or ecological issues. 'Ecological citizenship' and 'citizen education' are discussed by Dobson (2004) who refers to our rights, responsibilities and obligations as citizens. He also points to the importance of identifying cases of environmental justice.

3   The idea of speaking about 'ideology' and ideological orientation in connection with business companies may appear strange to some readers. In business management literature, more precisely organization theory, one can find signs of a new thinking in this respect. In their book *Rethinking Organizational Behaviour*, Jackson and Carter (2000) regard 'ideology' as ubiquitous and even connect ideology and decision-making in a manner not very different from mine.

Further readings

How do we understand individuals and organizations in the economy? From a positivistic point of view this becomes a question of truth and the best explanation of how individuals and organizations behave. Is egoism the best possible approximation of reality? Are companies only focusing on shareholder value?

In his early book *Administrative Behaviour* (1947), Herbert Simon, much like institutionalists, pointed to the role of habits in economic affairs and to 'bounded rationality'. Contrary to neoclassical assumptions, information is normally limited, search processes may be initiated and search costs are considered as part of rationality. In 1988 Amitai Etzioni's book *The Moral Dimension: Toward a New Economics* was published where he pointed to an 'I and we paradigm'. Individuals are both considering their own interests and those of different others (we-categories). Mary E. Clark points in a similar direction in her two books *Ariadne's Thread. The Search for New Modes of Thinking* (1989) and *In Search of Human Nature* (2002). She emphasizes 'bonding' as an important, if not dominant, feature both in the human and non-human world.

As I see it, the neoclassical idea of a 'rational egoist' is a model with serious limitations since it tends to be too far from realities in most situations of economic behaviour. At issue is instead what kind of mixture between egoistic and other-related behaviour one can expect. But choosing one model rather than another is not just a matter of being close to reality. There is a normative content in each model and preference for one model can as well be seen as a political and ideological act. We potentially influence others by the models we use. Will we get a better world by assuming that all individuals are born egoists, for example?

Questions for discussion

➤ What is your preferred model of individuals in relation to attempts to get closer to an SD path? Do you see yourself and your fellow human beings as egoists moving around in the market place or as persons with divergent but also many kinds of common interests?

➤ Neoclassical microeconomics only considers 'firms' among organizations. Why do you think other kinds of organizations are excluded from consideration? Do non-business organizations have a role in the development dialogue?

Interpretations of Non-Market and Market Relationships in Relation to Sustainability

The only kind of relationships dealt with in neoclassical textbooks is market relationships and markets are interpreted mechanistically in terms of supply and demand. The focus is on one commodity at a time. This commodity is supplied by one or more firms and demanded by consumers. This is presented in diagrams with prices of the commodity on the vertical axis and quantity on the horizontal axis. It is argued that balance or equilibrium of price and quantity exchanged is reached where the total supply (from all firms producing the commodity) intersects with the total demand from all consumers (or others purchasing the commodity). The diagram refers to a point in time. The equilibrium may be disturbed by changes in demand, supply or both, and a new equilibrium point (price and quantity exchanged) will emerge.[1]

The model in terms of supply and demand helps demonstrate the functioning of some markets. The point here is that the neoclassical model is just one possibility and other models may be equally, or more relevant for understanding the functioning of markets (see Figure 5.1). It is also argued that relationships of a non-market nature are relevant for understanding an economy in relation to sustainability issues. Reference can be made to a social embeddedness of the market and the economy. The market is part of society rather than being separate and separable from it. And the market can be interpreted in social and cultural terms as emphasized earlier.

Ideological implications of the supply and demand model

The tendency of neoclassical economists, and many of their followers, to interpret all kinds of relationships in market terms and in terms of mechanistic models of supply and demand may appear innocent but can have significant ideological implications:

- This interpretation is often criticized as 'commodification' of the world and the economy; each diagram refers to one commodity and nothing more.

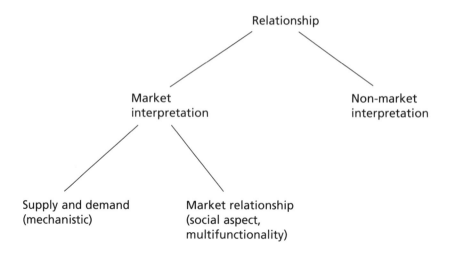

Figure 5.1 *Relationships can be interpreted in market or non-market terms; there can also be different types of market interpretations*

Source: Söderbaum (2005, p96)

- The focus is on the monetary aspect of supplying and demanding the commodity; consumers (buyers) are assumed to focus on price (for a given quality of commodity) and producers or suppliers are assumed to focus on monetary costs of producing and selling the commodity. This simplification is clearly a case of 'monetary reductionism'.
- Supply and demand are regarded as 'forces' in a mechanistic sense. This downplays or excludes all kinds of ethical and ideological aspects of market actors' thoughts and behaviour.
- The neoclassical idea of efficiency is closely connected with the mentioned commodification and monetary reductionism of supply and demand theory. Producing and selling a commodity at lower price is a sign of increased efficiency.
- In neoclassical environmental economics reference is made to externalities and the 'polluter pays principle'. The theory only deals with one externality at a time, compared with the complexity of impacts in most production and trade situations. In his book *The Social Costs of Private Enterprise* (1950), K. William Kapp argued at an early stage that negative external impacts should not be seen as exceptional cases. In the ambition to reduce costs, business companies look for opportunities to shift negative (monetary and non-monetary) impacts to others (Kapp, 1950). Moreover, the neoclassical idea of 'appropriate correction' for third party impacts is ideologically specific. This excludes a number of other ideological options. Future generations and non-human forms of life may also be affected as

'third parties', making the neoclassical pretension of correct solutions misleading.

- There is certainly some room for market interpretations and even for the supply and demand model (currency markets being one example) but the present tendency to extend the supply and demand market interpretation to all kinds of phenomena is highly ideological. For example, will we get a better world by exchanging 'pollution rights' for CO_2 or 'water use rights' (Simpson and Ringskog, 1997) in markets? We are back to neo-liberalism and the close relationship between neoclassical economics and neo-liberalism as ideology.
- Monetary reductionism at the micro level paves the way for monetary indicators such as GDP at the macro level. Thus, market ideology, in the form of supply and demand models, is closely related to GDP-growth ideology. Exclusive reliance on GDP indicators is far from the multidimensional idea of SD previously emphasized.

An alternative interpretation of market relationships

For that part of activities where markets can play a positive role, models of market exchange other than the supply and demand model can be considered (see Figure 5.1). A relationship between two market actors takes place in a social and institutional context and just as the institutional context has its history, the same is true of the relationship (see Table 5.1). Is there a well-functioning, ongoing institutional context that facilitates market activities? What are the background factors of the present relationship between the market actors? Are personal and social experiences involved as part of the market transaction?

Each market transaction is similarly 'embedded' in a physical and ecological context and this context is normally affected by the transaction. For 'sustainability economics', obviously ecosystems represent an important part of the context. Production and marketing processes use raw materials and natural resources as inputs. On the output side, pollution is part of that which is 'produced'.

The behaviour of market actors is specific with respect to place, ways of communicating and so on. Rather than understanding individuals in terms of NEM assumptions, reference is made to a PEP (see Table 5.1). Similarly, organizations, as market actors, are understood in political terms as PEOs. The market is then seen as a multifaceted relationship between market actors, where social aspects and history play a role. As an example, business-to-business market relationships are often better understood if one focuses on how market actors relate to each other through commitments, trust and so on (Ford, 1990), rather than exclusively on commodities sold and bought at specific prices.

Table 5.1 *Two interpretations of 'market' as a phenomenon*

Aspects compared	Neoclassical	Institutional
History	Not considered relevant	History relevant; path-dependence, etc.
Relevant context ('embeddedness')	Markets for commodities and factors of production	Social, institutional (e.g., market), ecological embeddedness
View of individual	NEM	PEP as market actor
View of organization	Profit-maximizing firm	PEO as market actor
Interaction between buyer and seller	Supply and demand	Multifaceted relationship between potentially responsible actors
Goods and services	Homogeneity; one commodity at a time	Also heterogeneity, multiple commodities and transactions, multifunctionality
Availability of knowledge and information about values, alternatives and impacts	Complete information assumed	Incomplete, normally fragmentary and sometimes contradictory knowledge and information; search activities common
Motives for transaction	Profits and utility related to quantity and price (optimization)	Ideological considerations; monetary price and beyond ('matching' ideological orientation and expected impacts)
Ethical/ideological position	Emphasis on personal gain (belief in 'invisible hand')	Open-ended; also inclusive (I and we paradigm, 'person in community')
Features of relationship	Independence; contract between parties with conflicting interests	Independence or cooperation an open issue; trust, fairness, justice potentially considered

According to the alternative view, the market is understood as being within the political sphere. Market actors are political actors with specific responsibilities and may be held accountable for their actions as part of a democratic society. The lifestyles of individuals as consumers, citizens and in other roles become a potential political issue. The same is true for corporations as producers and users of different commodities. The issues of CSR, EMSs, environmental labelling, fair-trade labelling, life cycle analysis (LCA) and EIAs become understandable as part of this theoretical perspective. They are largely incompatible with neoclassical theory.

The PEP and PEO models and the market model indicated should be understood as ideologically open models that allow both for new thinking and new values for individuals and for the possibility of individuals and organizations with a narrow ethical and ideological view. The models are at the same time normative in the sense that they encourage debate and scientific investigation about how individuals and organizations relate to the larger democratic society.

There are markets where it is fair to assume that the commodities produced and exchanged are homogeneous but many producers try to differentiate their products from competitors and the relationships between two market actors may refer to more than one commodity and to multiple transactions. Each transaction (or set of transactions) has multiple impacts that can be understood in multifunctional terms. If market actor A chooses to buy a product from market actor B rather than market actor C, this may have important impacts beyond delivery of the product at a price. The idea that all impacts are well reflected in monetary costs and prices (even after corrections for externalities) is strange and out of touch with reality. For example, international trade in agricultural products may affect employment at different places, local cultures, etc. Many stakeholders, interested parties and actors may be involved and have an opinion. Models that somehow allow for these complexities are needed. The mistakes of neoclassical economists, as elsewhere, are twofold. First, impacts cannot satisfactorily be expressed in monetary terms (monetary reductionism). Second, values and ideological orientation of affected and concerned persons cannot be reduced to one correct method of valuation (with connected prices) from the point of view of societal resource allocation ('ideological reductionism').

Only one more of the comparative criteria from Table 5.1 will be commented upon, the assumptions made about the availability of knowledge and information for market actors. In neoclassical theory of the textbook version, 'perfect information' is normally assumed. Preferences of consumers are assumed to be known, as is the objective function of firms. Similarly, available alternatives and impacts are known to the market actors. Institutional economics (right-hand side of Table 5.1) starts with the opposite assumption. It is assumed that available knowledge and information is always incomplete and fragmentary. The transaction is part of an ongoing evolutionary process where the search for additional knowledge and information and the reconsideration of one's ideological orientation (an organization's mission statement) is always an option. Search processes sometimes lead to innovations of a social, institutional or product-related kind that redefine the market situation and the ideas about desirable partners within the market or for other cooperation.

A frame of reference for sustainability politics

The assumptions about individuals as PEPs, organizations as PEOs and about market and non-market relationships can now be brought together in a conceptual framework for sustainability politics (see Table 5.2).

The neoclassical perspective focuses on the national government and potential regulatory measures. In relation to (what is understood as) the economy, the state is the main political actor. Politicians may belong to different political parties and have different opinions but environmental or sustainability politics is connected with laws and other state regulation. This implies that politics is essentially channelled through the state administration. A distinction is made between 'command and control' instruments (prohibitions) and 'market-based instruments' (MBIs), where the former are generally dealt with in a derogatory manner and the latter preferred for ideological reasons as being more flexible. (If you do not want to take the full responsibility for your contribution to CO_2 emissions, you can buy pollutions rights in the market place, for instance.)

Table 5.2 *Sustainability politics: Roles of different actor categories*

	Neoclassical economics	Institutional economics
State	The state is the main actor; MBI versus 'command and control'	The state is the main actor but there are other political actors/policy-makers as well who influence state regulation, and initiate, and implement institutional change processes
Organizations/ business	Profit maximization; adaptation to new state regulation	PEO assumptions; a company may act as policy-maker by changing its mission statement and behaviour, and adapting to new regulation. Institutional change processes may be initiated and influenced
Organizations/ non-business	(Not part of neoclassical theory)	PEO assumptions; these organizations may act as policy-makers by changing their mission statements and behaviour, and adapting to new regulation. Institutional change processes may be initiated and influenced
Individual	Consumer maximizing utility; adaptation to new state legislation	PEP assumptions; individuals may act as policy-makers by changing their ideological orientation and behaviour, and adapting to new regulation. Institutional change processes may be initiated and influenced

As part of the neoclassical perspective, the main responsibility for sustainability politics is with the national government and state administration. Business organizations and consumers are expected to comply with existing state legislation and nothing more. Non-business organizations are non-existent as part of this perspective.

The right-hand side of Table 5.2 points to a more complex picture of relationships and responsibilities. Indeed, all actors whether individuals, business organizations or non-business organizations are regarded as policy-makers and have social responsibilities that extend beyond their own perceived self-interests. Individuals are responsible in all their roles and relationships as professionals, citizens, family members, etc. and have to consider their decisions and lifestyles, for example in relation to their understanding of SD. Similarly, organizations of the business and non-business kind are part of society and are responsible and accountable for their behaviour and impact on society at large. Concepts such as CSR are relevant as part of this perspective. On the non-business side, it becomes relevant for example to speak of a university social responsibility (USR) in relation to the sustainability challenge (Söderbaum, 2007c).

Policy-making is no longer seen as something that exclusively is a matter of government intervention. All (individuals and organizations as) actors are policy-makers and can try to influence both national policy and local government policy. They can articulate and implement their own sustainability policy by participating in public debate, cooperating with other actors and changing their behaviour. A learning process and power game is going on in society that not only affects the choice between 'command and control' instruments and MBIs to achieve given objectives but also the objectives themselves, or expressed in more general terms, the ideological orientation of national sustainability politics.

PEP assumptions suggest that each individual can be regarded as a policy-maker and even politician. While there is path-dependence, the individual has some freedom to choose positions and move in relation to a context that may be stable or changing. In moving in relation to her context, the individual at the same time influences the context of others and may contribute to institutional change processes at a collective level. Even decisions that may be considered trivial, such as participating in public debate concerning a local issue or reading a book can be interpreted in political terms. And as the reader has noted, one of the storylines of this book is to strengthen democracy by encouraging individuals to participate as individuals and part of groups or networks in political life.

Notes

1   The author apologizes for not reproducing the usual supply and demand diagram here. The reasons are twofold. Too many diagrams of this kind have been reproduced over the years (when compared with other ways of understanding markets). I also do not want to mislead potential readers who when seeing such diagrams may get the impression that the book only repeats familiar neoclassical ideas.

Further readings

Markets are essential for the functioning of an economy but expanding the role of corporations and markets at the expense of democracy and (national and local) government is not necessarily a good thing. *Rolling Back the Market. Economic Dogma and Political Choice* is the title of a book by Peter Self (2000) where he warns against the present expansion of corporations and markets in various parts of the world. The neoclassical idea of efficiency is just one among many possibilities and not a very attractive one.

Milton Friedman can be seen as the number one advocate of market expansion. His book *Free to Choose* (Friedman and Friedman, 1980) has been influential in many circles. Friedman emphasizes the freedom of some market actors while neglecting impacts upon (freedoms of) other market actors and actors in non-market roles. In relation to environmental issues, neoclassical economists such as Pearce and Turner (1990) and Pearce and Barbier (2000) in their books *Economics of Natural Resources and the Environment* and *Blueprint for a Sustainable Economy* respectively, similarly prefer MBIs to correct for observed market failures. Attempts to deal with climate change through the Kyoto Protocol are an example of this.

Models of markets and models of companies are closely related. From a sustainability point of view, companies have to move in a multidimensional direction where ethics and ideology are considered. But present laws represent an efficient barrier for such thinking and action according to Joel Bakan in his book *The Corporation. The Pathological Pursuit of Profit and Power* (2004). Only that which can be motivated by shareholder financial interests can be defended. David Vogel presents a similar but more many-sided view in his book *The Market for Virtue. The Potential and Limits of Corporate Social Responsibility* (2005).

Questions for discussion

➤ Will corporations and markets bring us closer to sustainability within the scope of present institutional framework and dominant economic theory and ideology? If not, what kind of change is necessary as you see it?

➤ The concept of 'market' can be understood in more ways than one. Will reasoning in terms of PEPs and PEOs as market actors bring us closer to SD?

➤ CSR is discussed extensively but what about non-business organizations? Do you agree that it is time, for example, to discuss USR or do you think that university scholars automatically do what is best from a sustainability point of view? Most universities are not restricted by considerations of shareholder value but there may be other barriers.

Actors, Agendas and Arenas for Social and Institutional Change

In Chapters 1 and 2, a radical interpretation of SD was advocated. A conceptual framework that may facilitate the desired transformation was offered in Chapters 3, 4 and 5. At issue is how this conceptual framework can be used to better understand and influence social and institutional change processes. Let us first, as part of the comparative approach of this study, try to get some idea of how these issues are approached in neoclassical economics.

While the neoclassical approach is essentially one of standing outside and looking for inefficiencies from a societal point of view (based upon neoclassical conceptual and ideological ideas of 'efficiency'), our approach will be more actor-oriented. How do actors in different roles interpret SD? How does this understanding affect actors' behaviour and practice? Are there strategies and models that can be used to encourage actors to behave and decide in a manner that is conducive to SD?

As part of the market and GDP-growth ideology, entrepreneurs who start new business activities are celebrated. We can ask whether a different kind of change agent or entrepreneur, 'entrepreneurs for sustainability', deserve the same attention. Is there a need for different and broader ideas of efficiency? Are the sustainability dimensions of entrepreneurship even more important than the conventional dimensions in terms of profits and contribution to GDP growth? How do individuals and organizations engaged in business and non-business activities relate to the sustainability challenge?

The neoclassical approach to social and institutional change processes

As previously indicated, neoclassical economists tend to see 'economic growth' in GDP terms as the main indicator of performance of an economy.[1] Welfare improvements tend to be regarded as a matter of GDP growth. With increased production, more financial resources will be available, more will be invested, more will be consumed and the economy will 'prosper', etc. The 'market mechanism' is considered to be the main instrument in achieving improved welfare in this sense. It is also admitted that markets can fail; the same is true of governments. 'Market failures' refer to situations with negative externalities (i.e. negative impacts upon parties who are not directly involved in a market transaction). The government can apply the PPP, it is argued, to correct this situation. This implies that those who benefit from the transaction should pay a price in monetary terms for the damage inflicted upon third parties. The government may similarly fail by financially supporting activities that cause damage to specific parties or society at large and, again, this can be corrected by abandoning the same financial support.

This reliance on economic growth and markets means that the neoclassical economist does not tend to take the present debate about SD seriously. At best, 'economic growth' is modified to become 'sustainable (economic) growth', suggesting that there is some room for adjustments in incentive systems based on social and environmental considerations. The market is still viewed as the main vehicle and beliefs connected with the superiority of markets are so strong that only marginal corrections in the form of environmental charges can be considered. Since environmental problems are ubiquitous, a serious application of the PPP would bring us close to a kind of planned economy, implying that the government has to correct almost all prices. This would not be compatible with the market ideology espoused in the first place by most neoclassical economists. There is also an issue of compensation. In the case of environmental effects, many parties (in the extreme case, all inhabitants on Earth) can normally claim compensation. Is it at all reasonable in such cases to think of compensation in monetary terms? How do we account for the interest of future generations where there is irreversible damage?

This means that the idea of social change, as part of neoclassical economics, is mainly a matter of market adjustments within the scope of existing institutions. The impersonal forces of supply and demand determine the future of an economy. Firms look for opportunities to make profits and consumers buy commodities to maximize their utility. There is no need for new thinking in terms of paradigms or ideologies. The state provides an infrastructure for consumers and producers, and competitiveness of industry at the regional and national levels is all that matters and is regarded as the road to prosperity.

Understanding social and institutional change processes

The purpose of this book is to understand 'sustainability economics', i.e. an economics that has a better chance than neoclassical economics to guide us towards SD. One essential part of a sustainability economics is to understand institutional change processes that will either bring us closer to or further away from SD. Examples of 'institutions' that are judged to play a negative and positive role will be provided.

The conceptual framework and discourse about interpretations of SD already presented are part of a broad perspective on social and institutional change processes. The following elements of such a broad perspective are suggested:

- An actor-oriented perspective based on a model of the individual as an actor guided by an ideological orientation (PEP) and the organization as actor (PEO) guided by a mission statement.
- A recognition of the existence of competing perspectives or worldviews in a broad sense (theory of knowledge, paradigms in economics, ideologies and ideological orientations) with connected social and political movements.
- Closely related to the above broad perspectives are a number of more action-oriented models or strategies for social and institutional change. These models point to specific interpretations of various phenomena (not only models of individuals and organizations, but also models of markets, models for accounting at the organizational and societal level, models of education and learning for SD, models for certification schemes, etc.).
- Change in a desired direction at the micro level of individuals and organizations or at the societal level is not always easy. A way of looking at inertia and its opposite, flexibility, is needed.
- A perspective, in a more limited sense, is needed that refers to the emergence and development of specific institutions. Do they appear as a result of 'forces' in a mechanistic sense or are they planned and initiated by human actors? In the latter case it becomes relevant to identify actors that qualify as 'entrepreneurs for sustainability' as well as 'innovations for sustainability' of a social and institutional kind.
- Ideas about how institutions interact and how existing institutions affect the possible emergence of new ones.
- An understanding of the role of public dialogue in relation to institutional inertia and change.

Models of the individual and organizations as actors (PEPs and PEOs) were presented in Chapter 4 and perspectives in a broad sense, referring to the role of science in society, paradigms in economics and ideology were outlined in Chapter 3. Different interpretations of SD were also offered. These broad perspectives can of course be identified and presented in other terms. The important thing is to realize that science and ideology play a role in political and institutional change processes and that a power game is going on between advocates of different perspectives in this broad sense.

In social and institutional change (and opposition to change) models of a more targeted and specific kind also play a role. Such models or strategies for change are presented in the next section. Another section follows that provides examples of the emergence of new institutions and modification of existing institutions.

Models and strategies for sustainable development

Who are the actors that can actively contribute to SD? What are the options for an actor that wishes to contribute to SD in its ecological modernization or more radical sense? For example, individuals in their different roles as citizens, as professionals, as parents and as actors in the market place, can each play a role. Among organizations, universities, public agencies, regional development entities, business companies, trade organizations, churches and others can be active by reorienting their roles, ideologies and strategies. Just as a successful football-player is constantly on the move in relation to other players, experimenting with new positions and new roles is often a good idea in public life.

In this section, the discussion is limited to a list of models that each can play a role in influencing social and institutional change (c.f., Söderbaum, 2000, pp119–126). Each model of understanding social and institutional change processes can be used for the purpose of formulating strategies. The models and strategies listed can also be used in combination:

- paradigm and ideology development model;
- learning and education model;
- public debate model;
- decision-making model;
- monitoring, accounting and reporting model;
- political declaration and legal model;
- actor-network and social movement model;
- organizational and institutional change model;
- models for certification and evaluation by external actors;
- market model;
- labelling and listing model;
- technology development model;
- demonstration and 'good practice' model;
- other models.

Many assume that science (for example paradigms in economics) already exists and that ideologies have been developed in previous centuries, making them fixed and immovable. This is simply not true. While there is considerable inertia, it is equally true that paradigms and ideologies change at the level of the individual and in society at large. This 'constant change' means that one can get further away from or closer to SD in a specific sense. *Paradigm and ideology development* is probably one of the most important single (sets of) factors that can play a decisive role. The road to a better society and improved decision-making is not only a matter of improved estimates of impacts for given alternatives of choice. Also ideologies can be improved in terms of seriously considering environmental and development issues. With a clarified ideological orientation, better alternatives of choice will emerge and be articulated and new impact profiles will become possible.

It is a mistake to regard the issue of ideology as being exclusively a matter for politicians. Scholars and civil servants should take an interest in issues of ideology and politicians should, for the same reasons, not lay the responsibility for development of disciplinary and interdisciplinary paradigms exclusively on the shoulders of university scholars. The previously discussed idea that a clear separation can be made between politics and science may have good intentions but can also pave the way for monopoly in science. This is demonstrated by the case of neoclassical economics.

The mentioned 'paradigm and ideology development model' can be seen as a meta-model for some of the more specific approaches to be discussed. This is also true for a *learning and education model*. We need improved paradigms and we need to clarify a constructive SD ideology as something by itself and in relation to more conventional political ideologies. Theoretical and ideological perspectives are not enough. University professors and other actors as professionals, politicians, parents, etc. have increasingly to internalize these values through learning in a broad sense. Agreeing 'in theory' does not, as we all know, mean that changes in practice will follow. As an example, EPI is accepted as principle but not much has happened so far in practice. Broad acceptance of a principle such as EPI in a population of actors is still an important step.[2]

Those of us who believe in democracy tend to think that public dialogue is important. Actors who wish to influence societal change often rely on a *public debate model*. Participation in public debate depends on the availability of infrastructure in terms of newspapers, newsletters, websites, television channels, journals, etc. It also depends on the willingness of those who control public arenas to listen to many voices. This makes the imperatives of democracy of crucial importance. While public debate can be manipulated in many ways, those who wish to work for SD have to look for open, rather than closed, doors. It appears that recent development of information technology (IT) has increased the number of opportunities in a positive sense.

A *decision-making model* that is compatible with the ideas of SD has to be developed and used. Decision-making can no longer be based on simplistic ideas of monetary performance. Environmental, social and cultural performance are also parts of SD and the important thing is to make all kinds of impacts visible, rather than hide them behind one-dimensional numbers. The ethical, precautionary and democratic aspects of SD also have to be dealt with, as is further discussed in Chapter 7 on sustainability assessment.

Progress towards a sustainable society has to be measured in some way. This means that there is a role for a *monitoring, accounting and reporting model*. Environmental and social indicators should be used with the more conventional economic indicators. Our previous distinction between non-monetary flows and non-monetary positions is relevant here (see Table 2.1). Has environmental performance been improved or not? What happens to the state (or position) of the environment? As mentioned earlier, in the case of Sweden, 16 groups of environmental objectives have been formulated at the national level and attempts are now being made to make these indicators operational at the regional level. Also, changes in the 'positions' of individuals and organizations in relation to SD deserve attention. Are they taking steps in the right direction?

Knowing where you stand is normally a good thing. It means that an aspiration level and, in a more general sense, objectives can be formulated and results reported for organizations, municipalities, regions, etc. It is quite probable that broadening the scope of accounting and reporting activities to become more in line with SD evaluation will influence the ideological orientation and objectives of individuals and organizations.

Social change processes can also be related to political declarations and such declarations often initiate legal measures of one kind or another. Reference can be made to a *political declaration and legal model*. As examples of political declarations, SD is accepted as an objective at the UN level, for the EU, for Sweden as a nation, for Mälardalen as a region and for Västerås and Uppsala as municipalities or cities. For the EU, EPI is an important vision as previously mentioned. Although attempts have been made to define SD and EPI, the interpretation differs to some extent and legal action is lagging behind. Political declarations of this kind are still of importance in the sense that it has become legitimate in many contexts to raise social and environmental issues and to expect action. Dialogue is a precondition for social and institutional change processes.

An *actor network (and social movement) model* points to situations where actors get together to work for SD in a more or less radical sense. Individuals learn from each other and one individual may accept the authority of another. This model (as other models discussed here) builds on PEP assumptions. Reference can be made to opinion leaders and other kinds of leadership based on authority. As previously discussed, actors who share a green ideological orientation may cooperate in networks to change society in a desired direction. This can bring us to an *organizational and institutional change model*. Those who share a similar ideological orientation and similar interests can get together and build organizations to further their interests and increase the number of supporters. One special case of organizational arrangement is to apply a *model for standardization and certification*, which includes *evaluation by external actors*. As examples, ABB, a business corporation, and Mälardalen University have become certified according to ISO 14001.

While neoclassical economists almost exclusively point to *market models*, our list is more comprehensive. Market models are also important in the present theoretical perspective, although our view of markets is not limited to the supply and demand models of neoclassical economics (see Figure 5.1 and Table 5.1). Rather than assuming that the objectives of market actors are given, we are interested in how the ideological orientation of market actors may change and how one market actor interacts with another actor in a purposeful learning process. The PPP referred to by neoclassical economists is still useful in influencing market behaviour. The problem is that it is seldom applied in practice. This has to do with the limitations of the neoclassical paradigm and the kind of market ideology generally advocated by neoclassical economists and many others. Also, special market arrangements for pollution permits and other similar tools may have a role, although I am personally 'less than enthusiastic' about such possibilities. Given the dominance of a market ideology in our societies, which sometimes can be referred to as 'market fundamentalism', there may be a role, at least in the short run, for new kinds of markets where rights to pollute are traded. But I believe that the long-run objective must be one of 'rolling back' the market (Self, 1993, 2000) to increasingly rely on other models of social change. One case in point is Larry Lohman's critical assessment of the Kyoto Protocol with its 'flexible mechanisms' concerning greenhouse gases (Lohman, 2006).

Individuals and organizations as actors have ideological orientations and look for behavioural alternatives, product alternatives, investment alternatives, employment alternatives or partners that fit into their ideological orientation. Some parts of behaviour are habitual and other parts are more open to new thinking and new information. In this situation, search and decision-making can be facilitated by reference to a *labelling and listing model*. Actors can look for green labels or fair-trade labels to the extent that they support the SD idea. They can scrutinize lists of chemicals or materials that have been classified as toxic or otherwise dangerous from the point of view of health or environment. Also, the functioning of markets can be improved to the extent that market actors become well informed about such dysfunctional properties of goods and services.

New technology plays an important role in society, making a *technology development model* relevant to our ideas about social and institutional change processes. Some actors are very optimistic about new technology as an automatic problem solver to all kinds of societal problems. As in the case of markets, I am more cautious. Just as markets and technology can play important roles in attempts to get closer to SD, the opposite may also be true. It all depends on the ideological orientation of the actors engaged in technological research and development, and on the ideological orientation of market actors. The cultural and institutional context will also play a role. This means that neither the market nor new technology in isolation will be enough to solve present problems. The issues of ideology and paradigms have to be involved.

Finally, a *demonstration and 'good practice' model* has been identified. This can be seen as part of the previous learning and education model. Individuals can learn from each other at both a theoretical level and from cases of good practice. The same is true of business companies, public agencies and municipalities. Cases of good governance can supply ideas to be used in other places. This is precisely one of the main ideas of the European Regional Sustainable Development Network mentioned in the Preface to this book. Are there cases of good practice in Västmanland or Mälardalen, my 'home region', that can be copied or otherwise stimulate new thinking in other regions? What can we in Västmanland (Mälardalen) learn from theoretical and practical work going on in other participating regions of the network?

The list of models to be used as a basis of strategy formulation can certainly be extended and other lists may be as meaningful. We could, for example, have referred to democracy as a meta-model and then related some of the other models to the democracy model. Another comment relates to the relationship between models. Taking the example of EMSs, such as ISO 14001 or the Eco-Management and Auditing Scheme (EMAS) of the EU, it is clear how these systems combine a number of the models discussed. There is an important education element in ISO 14001 and in EMAS. They also employ a system of accounting, reporting and certification. Although EMSs of the present kind essentially belong to the 'ecological modernization' category in terms of paradigm and ideology, they can at least contribute to a more open dialogue about company objectives and responsibilities.

Inertia and flexibility

While language, conceptual framework and ways of interpreting the world play an important role as part of social and institutional change processes, it would be a mistake to believe that change in a desired direction always takes place easily. History plays a role and the existence of path-dependence and various forms of inertia suggests that changing the direction of an ongoing development process is not easy. It can rather be very difficult at all levels from the individual to the group, the organization, the local community, the region to the national level and even more global level.

Why is it difficult? We can return to the protected or prohibited zones mentioned earlier. At any point in time, there are paradigms (in economics, for instance) that dominate, and ideologies that dominate with a prevailing institutional framework. This means that a large number, perhaps a majority of actors, find them 'natural' or satisfactory. The support for 'business as usual' as an ideological orientation is considerable in many societies and most people find only incremental change reasonable to accept. The idea of economic growth is modified to become 'sustained growth' and there are a number of vested interests at play that actively defend the status quo or the dominant direction of change.

Inertia (and its opposite, flexibility) can be discussed in relation to many kinds of dimensions. In an early study (Söderbaum, 1973, pp100–107), I suggested the following list:

- psychological dimensions;
- social dimensions;
- ethical-legal dimensions;
- aesthetic dimensions;
- physiological dimensions;
- biological, biochemical, ecological dimensions;
- physical-technical and physical-chemical dimensions;
- dimensions related to information and knowledge;
- spatial dimensions;
- dimensions related to historical objects or environments;
- monetary and market-related dimensions.

Changes in dimensions of this kind often go together and cannot easily be separated. Inertia of various kinds may counteract change desired by some actors or interested parties. Actors or interested parties who desire change in specific directions can work together to overcome inertia, i.e. increase flexibility for that kind of change and also try to consolidate or secure desired change through various commitments. Other actors with a different ideological orientation may attempt to obstruct or block the kind of change process desired by the first group. This can be understood as a power game between different groups who wish to influence societal and institutional change according to their respective ideological orientations. Each actor starts from a particular position and is thinking in terms of multiple steps towards a future desired position, which again becomes a starting point for the next move. Considering future options in this way can be compared to a game of chess. While the possible patterns of positional changes are limited in the case of playing chess, this is not so in real life. Not only familiar patterns but also new patterns may emerge as a result of interaction between different players.

This can be illustrated by way of a town planning example. In 1971, I wrote a newspaper article in the local newspaper, *Upsala Nya Tidning*, questioning a multi-storey car park being planned for the city centre. Adding one car park after another in this part of Uppsala was perhaps not a wise policy. I pointed to various forms of pollution from cars and suggested that this policy was perhaps not even good for the retail units that were supposed to benefit from the arrangement. I also suspected that commitments of various kinds would make it very difficult for those who wished to reverse the decision process. Contrary to my expectations, a leading politician responded to my article and argued that it was still possible to rethink plans for the site. The result was a different approach to the car planning issue.

In a case such as this, one can imagine that there are ideological and cognitive commitments made at an early stage, for example when a group of actors make a proposal and even more so when an architect is asked to suggest a design and make a first drawing. Social and political commitments may be added when politicians get involved. At some stage suppliers and construction companies are contacted that can lead to purchasing contracts and when construction work starts there is hardly any way out. Actors and interested parties who believe that they will benefit from a building do their best to push the process forward and make it more or less irreversible at an early stage. Normal rules of democracy may put up a temporary barrier to such attempts. In the mentioned case, the process was reopened and the development plans were reconsidered.

Examples of institutional change processes

As previously argued, an actor-oriented approach appears relevant to understanding institutional change processes. 'Actors' relate to each other in networks and organizations. They appear in 'arenas' to further their 'agendas' about desired institutional change or protection of present arrangements. Reference can thus be made to an actor–agenda–arena (AAA) approach. Normal imperatives of democracy play a role in this interaction, as do exploitation of power positions by influential actors.

The AAA approach points to the importance of ideological orientation and the theoretical perspectives or conceptual frameworks used by actors in interpreting various phenomena. Any attempt to get closer to an SD path will involve changes in conceptual framework, language and connected interpretations. This can be illustrated by reference to the example of an increased number of business companies being certified according to ISO 14001. The idea of a 'business company' with connected manifestations is in itself an 'institution' and many are those who interpret 'business company' as a 'profit-maximizing entity'. Neoclassical economics tends to strengthen this interpretation. Business management literature and journalism also point in this direction.

At some stage, as a result of the initiatives of some actors connected with business, EMSs such as ISO 14001 appeared on the scene as an 'institution' in itself. An increasing number of individuals understand the meaning of EMS and support the ideology behind it, then implying that the institution is strengthened. But the fact that some companies are certified according to ISO 14001 can actually change our understanding of the business companies being certified. A 'certified business company' can be interpreted as being different from companies that are not certified. The institution of 'business company' is then understood in broader terms. It is not only a matter of monetary profits but also of 'environmental performance'. One may speak of a tension or competition between the 'old' interpretation of business company and a newer one.

The following aspects of such institutional change processes are judged relevant:

- *interpretation* of a phenomenon among available interpretative options;
- *concepts* and models used for interpretation;
- *naming* the phenomenon together with terminology and language used;
- *other manifestations* of the phenomenon;
- *acceptance* of interpretation and manifestations (thereby *increasing legitimacy*) by an increasing number of actors.

A new interpretation plays a key role for the emergence of an institution but is just one among processes. An 'institution' becomes strengthened or established to the extent that the interpretation is shared and emotionally supported by an increasing number of actors and to the extent that it becomes manifested in symbols or concrete behaviour among an increasing number of actors. Through the mentioned processes, 'institutionalization' (or the opposite; de-institutionalization) may take place. Institutionalization refers to an institution that becomes emotionally and otherwise more established among actors. Deinstitutionalization refers to a situation where an institution loses support over time and eventually may become 'out-competed' or replaced by other institutions.

Let us take a look more closely at the case of EMSs. In business, financial management systems with connected accounting procedures have long been in existence. These systems are used to measure monetary performance in terms of flows (for example profits) and positions (for example balance sheets indicating assets and liabilities). It is clear, however, that business operations have a number of non-monetary impacts that are not easily visible in monetary accounting systems. For actors who wish to know and control what they are doing, ideas of non-monetary management systems of various kinds are not far-fetched.

Essential elements of financial management models could then be transferred to environmental management, albeit with difficulty. On the monetary side, accounting and auditing can refer to one-dimensional monetary interpretations while no one-dimensional indicator is available on the non-monetary side. Environmental impacts are multidimensional and often uncertain; the same is true of health impacts, social impacts and impacts on cultural heritage. In relation to this complexity, and for other reasons, the ambition of an EMS has become rather modest. One of the issues is whether an organization can show that its environmental performance has been improved in essential dimensions for a period, usually a year, compared with the previous period. Auditing organizations are created for independent control purposes and the EMS is named ISO 14001, thereby benefiting from the prestige and credibility of the International Organization for Standardization (ISO). If successful, the organization may receive a diploma and will be recognized through other manifestations of the system and specific persons may be appointed as environmental coordinators.

ISO 14001 may become more established and increase in popularity over time, or the opposite may be true. In some parts of the world, such as Northern Europe, the support for the system is considerable, while in the US, for example, thinking habits and ideological orientation point in a different direction. Our case also suggests that there is interdependence between institutions. The existence of ISO 14001 and other 'members' of the ISO 14000 family (ISO 14040 for LCA, ISO 14020 for environmental labelling) may, as we have seen, affect the understanding and interpretation of the 'business company' and its responsibilities.

Science and education is another area where institutional change processes can be observed. As an example, some leading ecologists initiated workshops in the 1980s and invited what they understood as leading environmental economists. The ecologists expressed scepticism concerning the ability of neoclassical economists to seriously handle environmental problems. Neoclassical environmental economics was judged to be less than adequate to constructively deal with the emerging problems. In 1989, a new organization was formed, the ISEE with its journal, *Ecological Economics*. Later, regional associations were added, such as the European Society for Ecological Economics (ESEE), the Russian Society, a society for Australia and New Zealand, the Canadian Society and the US Society, etc. Ecological economics became more institutionalized and respected over time through manifestations in the forms of the mentioned organizations, journals, articles, conferences, educational programmes at undergraduate and Master levels, professorships and more.[3]

It is not clear whether the ISEE or the regional societies play only a peripheral role or have a significant impact on policy-making and practice in different parts of the world. Politicians continue to largely rely on mainstream neoclassical economists with their simplistic recommendations to facilitate exports and GDP growth. The case of ISEE is also of interest because it indicates that similarity in interpretations (rather than identical interpretations) can be enough to strengthen an institution or set of institutions. Pluralism in conceptual framework and approach has become a way of handling tensions between natural scientists (who often limit their ideas about science to positivism) and economists with a social science background.

I will end this section of examples by pointing to some of the 'institutions' that I believe can play a positive role in relation to SD,[4] followed by a number of institutions that are more 'problematic'. On the positive side are:

- World Social Forum;
- certification schemes (ISO 14001, fair trade, etc.);
- *Post-Autistic Economics Review* (now *Real-World Economics Review*) and related books edited by Edward Fullbrook (2003, 2004, 2007);
- *Heterodox Economics Newsletter*;
- textbook projects for pluralistic economics;
- International Confederation of Associations for Pluralism in Economics;
- European Society for Ecological Economics with a newsletter, PhD courses, etc.;
- Green Economics Institute with the *International Journal of Green Economics*;
- Right Livelihood Award;
- publishing companies with a sustainability profile such as Earthscan, Zed Books, Greenleaf Publishing and many others.

On the negative side are:

- university departments of economics in most parts of the world with connected actors, textbooks, journals, etc.;
- neo-liberal think tanks in the US and Europe;
- the Bank of Sweden Prize in Economic Sciences in Memory of Alfred Nobel;
- WTO;
- present bonus systems for business CEOs;
- the limited liability doctrine regulating business corporations.

Of course, the lists can be extended. Reasons behind these lists can be found in other places in this book. Two comments will be made here. It is clear that the term 'institution' is used in a broad sense. Some define 'institution' as rules of the game and parts of a legal framework and prefer to make a distinction between 'institutions' in that sense and 'organizations'. I tend to include organizations among possible institutions. My way of using the word 'institution' can be interpreted as:

- a phenomenon that has a common understanding among a number of actors;
- individuals as actors relate to this phenomenon positively or negatively in cognitive and emotional terms through their ideological orientation;
- the phenomenon can be more or less established and protected through its name and various other manifestations;
- a phenomenon that can gain (or lose) in number of supporters over time (in relation to competing interpretations and institutions).

The existence of a 'common understanding' does not necessarily mean that the phenomenon is understood in exactly the same way. Rather the phenomenon is similarly understood by a number of persons. It is clear that many phenomena can be classified as institutions according to these criteria, and also that some ambiguity remains in this attempt at definition. A paradigm in economics (or an ideology such as neo-liberalism) qualifies as an institution. Even a highly visible and established person may match the criteria given. I do not see this as a significant problem.

My second comment has to do with interaction between institutions. It is clear that the institutions listed as positively contributing to SD mutually support each other and that the same is true of the institutions listed on the negative side. Abandoning the neoclassical monopoly at university departments of economics and reconstructing or dismantling the Bank of Sweden Prize in Economic Sciences in Memory of Alfred Nobel or the WTO would probably have positive repercussions in many directions.

A power game between groups with different ideological orientations

The AAA approach[5] can now be summarized as follows:

- PEP assumptions;
- the existence of inertia and path-dependence but also openings for change;
- emphasis on relationships between actors who, with their specific ideological orientation or agenda, appear in specific arenas;

- emphasis on the conceptual and interpretative aspect of 'ideological orientation';
- dialogue, search for consensus, conflict resolution and other aspects of interactive learning;
- 'institution' and 'institutional change' understood in interpretative, naming, manifestation, acceptance (legitimacy) terms;
- an assumption of heterogeneity in 'ideological orientation' in each conventionally defined actor category (such as farmers, business leaders, university scholars);
- an assumption that actors search for commonality in ideological terms by building networks and alliances within and across conventionally defined actor categories.

Only the heterogeneity assumption above will be further commented upon here. In neoclassical theory, more precisely 'public choice theory', an assumption of homogeneity is made concerning specific categories of actors such as farmers (Olson, 1965, 1982; Mueller, 1979). According to this theory, farmers are expected to collectively engage in rent-seeking activities based on common interests. This positivistic theory is of some interest but our more normative and interpretative approach suggests that differences within each category (farmers, bureaucrats or business leaders) are also relevant. Some farmers (business leaders) are concerned about environmental issues while others are not. Actors who have a similar ideological orientation but belong, in conventional terms, to different actor categories may work together as part of a common SD strategy (Söderbaum, 1991). Allowing for differences in ideological orientation among farmers as actors reduces the value of predictions based on public choice theory. 'Green' farmers differ from 'non-green' farmers and may cooperate in networks with 'green' bureaucrats to satisfy their own interests and get closer to common interests in terms of an SD path. Instead of focusing on actors in terms of professional categories, it is possible to focus on actor categories based on ideological orientation. The value of the AAA approach, with its 'heterogeneity principle', is then to critically scrutinize public choice theory and contribute to an improved understanding. The idea is no longer exclusively one of providing simplistic predictions.

In any society, or at least in our Western societies, some part of ongoing social and institutional change processes will bring us closer to an SD path. Other ongoing processes strengthen the unsustainable trends referred to earlier. While in the case of business companies, the addition of EMSs will bring us a little bit closer to SD (when compared to a situation where companies were not certified), the recent tendency to construct bonus systems for business CEOs based on prices in stock markets and the like may even add to the tendencies of short-sightedness and monetary reductionism.

There is no easy way out of this. The limited success of the EU principle of EPI, as reported by different authors in Lenschow (2002), should be understood in these terms of inertia in its different (multidimensional) forms. The conclusions are similar in a PhD study from Aalborg University (Bøgelund, 2003) where transportation policy in Denmark and Sweden is systematically compared in relation to the two theoretical perspectives of neoclassical environmental economics and ecological economics. The EPI idea of neoclassical environmental economics is connected with the PPP, while the approach of ecological economics is primarily focusing on environmental degradation and the formulation of targets in terms of environmental indicators and necessary measures to counteract this degradation. In her study, Bøgelund focuses on taxes and charges related to cars and her conclusion is that in the two countries, often claiming to be among the leaders in environmental policy, very little is happening. Neither in Sweden, where the transport dialogue is largely coined in the language of neoclassical (environmental) economics, nor in Denmark, where there is more room for an ecological economics perspective, does it seem appropriate to speak of an 'ecological rationality' gaining ground in relation to a traditional economic rationality with economic growth as the main objective (Bøgelund, 2003).

An empirical study of actors engaged in planning at the regional level carried out as part of the present research project unfortunately tells a similar story (Puskas Nordin et al, 2004). These actors were approached for a conversation about how they interpret SD and how such interpretations influence their role perceptions and practice as regional actors. How do environmental concerns enter into their activities?

Two regions were chosen for this study, Uppsala and Kalmar, the former region lies to the immediate north of Stockholm and the latter lies in the southeast of Sweden. In both regions organizations were recently established and reflect attempts to renew and strengthen planning activities. Thus one could expect that SD rather than GDP growth would represent a top priority on their agendas. In this respect, we were disappointed. Environmental issues certainly mattered for these actors and the regional bodies they represented but the traditional ideas of economic growth, entrepreneurship and innovations to strengthen competitiveness at the regional and international levels tend to be regarded as more important (and it is believed, or assumed, that any other problem will be resolved in this way). The stories told by these actors suggest that a lot remains to be done.

In understanding the limited success so far of the EPI principle at the EU level and for regional entities, our previous discussion about 'prohibited zones in the development dialogue' is useful. It is probably very illuminating to address the issues of inertia in terms of paradigms and related positions concerning theory of science, ideological orientation and institutions. The

number of actors who have internalized values connected with a radical interpretation of SD is still too small for the desired change in priorities to occur.

My own judgement is that economics has been at the heart of development
dialogue for so long that the dominance of neoclassical economics is an essential part of the problems faced. Since the Rome Treaty, European cooperation
has very much been understood as an 'economic' cooperation in a narrow
sense, guided by the principles and theories of neoclassical economics.
Economic growth in GDP terms is the single most important objective and
improving the functioning of the 'inner market' is now very much a mantra for
further growth and prosperity. I will not go into detail here about how the
'inner market' idea can be modified in the light of the previous discussion (see
Chapter 5). The first step is to allow for pluralism at university departments of
economics in the European Community. This does not appear to be an easy
step, considering the different kinds of inertia I have alluded to. A multi-
layered market system appears to be more useful and efficient in relation to the
ideas of SD advocated. Markets should be built from the local and regional
level and transportation of goods and people should not be allowed to increase
as is now the case. The current CAP has been much criticized and a new policy
should be based on the subsidiarity principle and mainly be seen as a regional
and national concern with some openings, of course, for international
exchange of goods and services.

Globalization in the sense of international dialogue and cooperation in the
fields of science and education or as cultural exchange is appreciated by most
people. So-called 'economic globalization' built on neo-liberalism and simplistic neoclassical trade theory is more of a problem. Local reintegration of
communities and markets seems to be a more promising vision. In their book
Green Alternatives to Globalisation, Woodin and Lucas (2004) suggest 'localization' and 'economic localization' as alternative buzzwords. Rather than only
criticizing what they dislike, they make a serious attempt to articulate visions
of a sustainable society and point to necessary institutional change.

National and local governments should be free to choose suppliers of
commodities as part of procurement policies, and tariffs and quotas should
again become an option in some situations. The reason is clear. The rules of the
WTO and EU (that largely follow the WTO recommendations) are built on
ideologically simplistic international trade theory. This theory focuses on price
of commodities traded while disregarding or downplaying all impacts of trade
upon nature and society. Should trade be built on huge differences in wages or
labour costs that may be temporary and reflect exploitation of the workers?
Can trade based on ignorance of health problems and natural resource degradation be called 'sustainable'?

The AAA model presented in this chapter can hopefully be used in
attempts to overcome some of the barriers and kinds of inertia discussed. It is

believed that research, education and public debate are necessary to achieve social and institutional change in specific directions. Actors in specific roles can 'make a difference'. Leadership is needed but so are social movements from below. The issue of ideological orientation and agenda setting in different arenas is central to any attempt to change society. Actors may cooperate and act in existing arenas. It is important to note that arenas (newspapers, television channels, etc.) may be controlled by groups that wish to avoid specific kinds of debate. In this situation, actors may need to establish new networks or arenas. The EU, as well as nations, should perhaps engage in multi-stakeholder dialogue to strengthen democracy also from the top down. Democracy is not something that already exists, it has to be regained and strengthened all the time at different levels. It is only in this way that it will be possible to counteract any tendencies for the power games going on in different arenas to be unequal in terms of resources, control and achievements.

Notes

1   It is true that neoclassical economists themselves may warn against this simplification. But since defending their paradigm seems more important, they have so far not shown any willingness to participate in the development of multidimensional indicator systems.
2   It is not necessarily so that acceptance of a principle comes first, followed by practice. Sometimes actors, more or less voluntarily, start practising things that later develop into habits and become accepted as principle.
3   This historical process has been critically described by Inge Røpke in two articles (2004, 2005).
4   The list of institutions that play a positive role can easily be extended and is somewhat arbitrary. The idea is only to encourage thinking about institutions and institutional change in these terms.
5   See also Söderbaum (2007b).

Further readings

Chapter 6 represents a move away from market-oriented ideas of social and institutional change to democracy-oriented ideas. The market is only part of a broader view where action based on other models of change is also considered.

In their book *Green Alternatives to Globalisation* (2004), Michael Woodin and Caroline Lucas present a radical view of necessary institutional change at the societal level. An account of historical institutional change in the scientific community is given in two articles 'The early history of modern ecological economics' and 'Trends in the development of ecological economics from the late 1980s to the early 2000s' by Inge Røpke (2004, 2005). Her study covers the early emergence of ecological economics and the establishment and 'institutionalization' of this field. Not only traditional scientific criteria but also ideology and power are involved in these attempts to move toward a sustainable society.

Questions for discussion

➤ In Chapter 6 examples of institutions that are judged to play a positive role for SD are given together with other institutions that are judged to play a more negative role. As reader, seeing the world from your vantage point, you may have a different opinion and can probably exemplify other institutions that play a positive or negative role.

➤ Make an attempt to describe an institutional change process that you have taken an interest in and is part of your experiences. Can you identify the different elements suggested for institutional change processes (interpretation, naming, manifestation and acceptance) in relation to your case?

7

Approaches to Decision-Making and Sustainability Assessment

Institutional economists emphasize the role of habits in economic behaviour. A large part of consumer behaviour, behaviour at the workplace and perhaps even investment behaviour, is habitual. Rules of thumb that have been established in the past facilitate life in many social and institutional contexts. This can be described as inertia or path-dependence. Searching for alternatives to habits can be costly in both non-monetary and monetary terms. Another aspect of human activity is best described as decision-making, i.e. conscious choice. By facing new alternatives with a different set of expected impacts, habits may be reconsidered and a learning process initiated, ending sometimes with new habits.

For some part of decisions at the level of the individual, the consequences of choosing one alternative rather than another is of little interest in relation to the larger society. But there are also cases where the choice made will affect others in important ways. The debate about SD suggests that even the choice of means of transportation to the workplace may affect others, even at a global level through CO_2 emissions.

In this chapter the focus is on approaches to decision-making at the level of projects, programmes and policies. Should a new road be built to connect two places or not, and if so, what are the alternatives to accomplish this task? Similarly, house construction, dam-building in a river and mining at a particular place are complex cases that deserve special attention. At the policy level, one may ask, for instance, if the EU should choose this or that environmental and development policy?

While the emphasis here is on public, political issues, it should be noted that a useful test of different approaches to decision-making and sustainability assessment is to consider if a proposed approach appears relevant and can be used also at the level of private decisions. Even private decisions can be complex with respect to impacts, ethical implications, uncertainties, etc. and our thinking and deliberations in relation to such complex decision situations are perhaps a source of learning for public decisions. Suggesting a completely different language and logic for public decisions (and even worse, a more simplistic logic as in the case of CBA) is perhaps not a wise strategy.

In some spheres of human life, people like to take risks. Gambling has become a growth industry. When an individual has political responsibilities for many others – as politician, administrator, business leader, etc. – we do not want her or him to refer to preferences for gambling and experiments based on limited knowledge and information. Instead, knowing as well as possible what you are doing beforehand becomes a virtue. The individual is an actor with certain responsibilities in a democratic society. All stakeholders and other concerned actors have a right to know about the ideological orientation referred to by the decision-maker(s) and about the expected impacts of competing alternatives.

Reference has been made to habits and I begin this chapter (as other chapters) by pointing to the neoclassical approach to decision-making at the societal level.

The neoclassical narrative: Cost–benefit analysis

The neoclassical approach to decision-making at the societal level is CBA. CBA is part of the positivist tradition in neoclassical economics. The economist is standing outside as an expert observing market prices and other phenomena. Based on such observations, he or she is expected to rank the alternatives considered by reference to numbers, usually so-called 'present values'. The CBA analyst is attempting to solve value issues in a value-neutral way.

This sounds like a contradiction. One cannot make recommendations about a 'best' alternative without referring to some values, or in our language, some 'ideological orientation'. Neoclassical economists try to solve this dilemma by dictating the kind of values or the ideology to be applied. They point to current market prices as a way to value the costs and benefits identified and sometimes to hypothetical market prices (when actual markets do not exist). The monetary dimension is assigned a central role to make one-dimensional calculations possible. It is simply assumed that all individuals in a society (usually a nation) agree about this way of evaluating alternatives, with its inbuilt ideology, to allocate resources. This assumption is not realistic today, if it ever has been (see discussion in Chapter 3).

The neoclassical approach to efficiency, rationality and decision-making is relatively consistent with a simplistic economic growth philosophy but does not go well with SD. If SD is multidimensional, as has been argued, and built on the idea that different types of impacts should be made visible, the attempt to capture all types of impacts in one-dimensional monetary (or other one-dimensional) terms is not very meaningful. If SD implies that issues of ethics and ideology should be illuminated rather than concealed, then the neoclassical idea of 'correct' ethics or ideology in the form of prices for purposes of 'efficient resource allocation' loses some of its attractiveness. If uncertainty and the application of a precautionary principle is taken seriously, then simplistic calculations of 'costs' and 'benefits' with unambiguous conclusions is not particularly helpful. If democracy is an essential element of SD, then reducing individuals to consumers and asking them for their 'willingness to pay' for specific commodities is no longer appropriate. Rather than listening obediently to the conclusions touted by experts, individuals as citizens and stakeholders should somehow be involved in the decision-making process.[1]

To become compatible with democracy and SD, an approach to decision-making has to be built on:

- disaggregation of impacts with respect to type and how they affect various groups;
- an open attitude to ethical and ideological issues;
- explicit consideration of risks and uncertainty;
- participation of stakeholders and other actors in illuminating and possibly influencing the decision-making process.

What are the alternatives to cost–benefit analysis?

There is more than one alternative to CBA. In Table 7.1, I compare CBA with positional analysis, my preferred approach to decision-making. Later on I also provide some comments about EIA, strategic impact assessment and multi-criteria approaches (MCA).

The left-hand side of Table 7.1 is essentially self-explanatory. As part of CBA, the analyst becomes an expert who claims to know about the impacts to be considered and how to value them in relation to each other. Money is the measuring rod. Expected future impacts are discounted to make them comparable with more immediate impacts. A present value is estimated for each alternative considered, making a ranking of alternatives possible. Politicians are expected to follow the analyst's recommendation about what is the best allocation of scarce resources. Since neoclassical economists can tell us what is best for society, there is little need for politicians. Technocracy becomes a substitute for democracy.

On the right-hand side of Table 7.1, there is still some role for technicalities but the main idea is to suggest an approach that is compatible with normal principles of democracy. In a democratic society, it is accepted and even encouraged that actors have different ideological orientations. There are, furthermore, political parties that differ with respect to ideas about progress in society and in specific policy domains. Tensions between advocates of different ideological orientations can be constructive and a source of new thinking. As part of an ongoing dialogue, opinions are sometimes reconsidered and a new

Table 7.1 *Comparing CBA with one possible alternative: Positional analysis*

	CBA	PA
Role of analyst	Expert, standing outside ('technocracy')	Facilitator, actor with specific responsibilities among other actors ('democracy')
Ethics and ideology	Specific market ideology applied	Articulation of competing ideological orientations, specific interpretations of SD included
Purpose of analysis	Clear-cut ranking of alternatives from a societal point of view (optimal solution)	Illuminate an issue with respect to ideological orientations, alternatives and impacts (conditional conclusions)
Role of politician or other decision-maker	Is expected to accept the conclusions of CBA study	Is expected to match his own ideological orientation with expected impacts of each alternative, being helped by the analysis carried out
Strategy to reach purpose	Money as the measuring rod. Discounting the future in monetary terms	Keeping monetary and non-monetary impacts separate. Impacts upon different groups and organizations kept separate (focus on inertia, path-dependence, irreversibility, conflicts and commonalities of interest)

partial consensus may emerge. SD, in the sense previously described as 'reasonable', may become accepted, for instance, by an increasing percentage of the population, including politicians and other influential actors.

The democracy argument is multifaceted. First, democracy is a meta-ideology in the sense that all citizens and organizations (PEPs and PEOs) have to accept it and live with it. It is a mistake, for instance, to argue that the market can replace democracy. Competition in the market place can have positive side-impacts on democracy when compared with a planned economy and dictatorship. However, it is a sign of wishful thinking (among neo-liberals, for instance) to assume that the neoclassical idea of markets and democracy are compatible. Too often the market goes against democracy and equality by concentrating power and resources in the hands of the few through monopolies and cartels. In spite of the recent debate about CSR, global corporations try to strengthen existing monopoly positions and search for new ones. This is essentially what so-called competition in the market place is about.

Second, the CBA analyst has no right to eliminate the existing diversity of ideological orientations or opinions (about a dam construction project, for instance) by referring to an alleged 'scientific' market ideology (except in the rare cases where all politicians and other actors agree about the CBA growth ideology). This suggests that a different set of roles should be attributed to analysts, politicians, stakeholders and other actors. On the right-hand side of Table 7.1, the analyst is referred to as a 'facilitator' (rather than 'expert' in a technocratic sense, as part of CBA) and is an actor with special competencies and responsibilities. The analyst should listen to and enter into a dialogue with stakeholders and concerned actors in a common problem-identifying and problem-solving process.

If there are competing ideological orientations among stakeholders and other concerned actors, then the analyst's first task is to articulate a limited number (for instance two or three) of such different ideological orientations. The conclusions made by the analyst will then be conditional in relation to each one of the ideological orientations articulated. It should be noted that a decision-maker such as a politician will refer to his own ideological orientation (or that of the group that she/he represents) rather than the typified ideological orientations used in the analysis. It is believed, however, that if the ideological orientations considered (much like the alternatives considered) clearly differ from each other (for example two extremes plus one intermediate version or compromise), then the decision-maker will normally find the analysis helpful to making a decision. The purpose of analysis in the case of PA is to 'illuminate' an issue (rather than 'solve' it in a technical way) for interested parties and concerned actors who differ with respect to their ideological orientation. The analyst is then listening to and cooperating with other actors and the analysis becomes an instrument of learning.

As mentioned before, PA is carried out in multidimensional terms. Monetary and non-monetary impacts are kept separate, as are different non-monetary impacts. It is argued that the logic on the non-monetary side differs from monetary analysis. Inertia, irreversibility and path-dependence should be illuminated rather than assumed away. Conflicts of interest should also be illuminated (rather than hidden) as a basis for conditional conclusions.

Positional thinking in non-monetary terms

PA includes systems thinking and conflict analysis among interdisciplinary approaches. Only 'positional thinking' is further commented upon here since it has given the name to the approach.[2] While CBA is normally described as a 'one-shot' analysis, PA is normally seen as a multiple-step approach (see Figure 7.1). From a starting position you can move in different directions. Each alternative first step will influence options at future points in time. Each move or alternative of choice will facilitate specific further moves and preclude other moves and positions.

In Figure 7.1, P_0 stands for the starting position of an object of description at time t_0. A_a and A_b are two alternatives considered at t_0. A_a is expected to lead to position P_{1a} at point in time t_1, while choosing A_b at t_0 will result in a position P_{1b} at t_1. P_{1b} differs qualitatively and quantitatively from P_{1a}. Assuming that A_a was chosen at t_0 then the options at t_1 will differ from the options at t_1 for the case that A_b had been chosen at t_0.

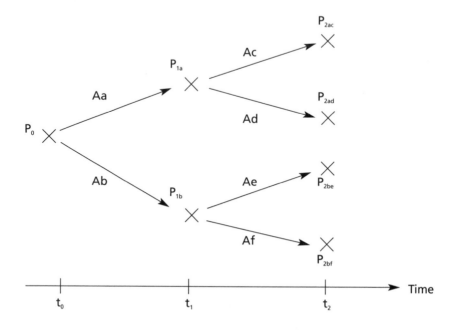

Figure 7.1 *Decision tree in positional terms*

Source: Söderbaum (1982b, p394)

This may sound both trivial and abstract. It is trivial in the sense of being close to our everyday experiences. If I have time to read one of two books during a particular period, my position in terms of knowledge and other experiences at the end of the period will differ depending on which one of the books I choose to read. Similarly, staying at home working in Uppsala for one particular day will probably lead to a different position at the end of the day from the option of commuting to my office in Västerås. Three slightly more complex decision situations are indicated in an attempt to illustrate why positional thinking is important.

Example 1: R&D option in business

In the middle of the 1960s, I was asked to assist a group of persons in charge of R&D projects in different companies (Pharmacia, a pharmaceutical company, and Fagersta, a steel manufacturer, among others). At the time, I was teaching marketing and consumer behaviour at the department of business studies, Uppsala University.

As discussed previously, business companies are responsible in monetary terms to shareholders and one strategy might be to focus directly on the expected contribution to monetary profits of each R&D project (programme) considered. What are the chances that a particular project will be successful in the sense of a new combination of technology and product? What are the market prospects for such a technology/product?

While monetary performance is always of importance, focusing directly on the monetary dimension may not be a wise strategy. One big issue for corporations choosing among R&D projects is uncertainty. Non-monetary impacts are sometimes less uncertain and estimating these impacts may provide a better idea of the monetary impacts. Rather than trying to estimate the contribution to monetary profits directly, moving in a multidimensional direction may improve the basis for decision-making. In addition to monetary impacts, the concept of 'stock of knowledge', more precisely stock of technical knowledge, was introduced. What is the stock of knowledge at t_0? What will the stock of knowledge be at t_1 for the case that A_a is chosen at t_0 and what will it be if A_b is chosen? Some important qualitative differences at t_1 can be expected. There may be differences in the monetary costs of carrying out A_a or A_b for the first period t_0–t_1 that can be relatively easy to estimate. But more interesting is that the expected stock of knowledge at t_1 will give us a hint about:

- the kind of R&D projects realistically possible at t_1 for the next move in period t_1–t_2;
- the monetary costs for each R&D option in period t_1–t_2. This monetary cost of adding specific pieces of knowledge will depend upon the (new) starting position at time t_1 in terms of available knowledge.

In this way, the difficult task of estimating the profitability of A_a and A_b at t_0 is replaced with an attempt to estimate intermediate outcomes in terms of stock of knowledge and the options that can be expected. From the cooperative project with representatives of business corporations a report *Profitability of Investments and Changes in Stock of Technical Knowledge*, was published in the form of a licentiate thesis in business economics at Uppsala University (Söderbaum, 1967). It is unclear whether the study had any significant impact upon decision-making in the participating companies but at least a forum for debate about the problems faced was established.

Inertia and irreversibility in terms of learning processes were issues raised in the R&D study. Investing in A_a will probably also lead to employment contracts with persons possessing other competencies than if A_b is chosen.

People are normally employed for a longer time than just one planning period. Families may move with those employed to a new place, etc.

Thinking in positional terms also points to the usefulness or benefits of enquiring into the starting position with respect to knowledge and resources of an organization. What are our strengths and weaknesses? Where do we already possess a competitive advantage in relation to other companies? How can we continue to strengthen the knowledge position in that same direction? Planning for R&D then becomes part of the broader strategic issues of mission statements and visions for the future.

Before moving to our next example, it may be of interest to ask how a typical neoclassical economist would look upon the issues raised. Many of these economists would deny that there is an issue at all. Reference can be made to the usual assumption of 'perfect knowledge' and to the one-commodity world of production functions in mathematical terms. Issues that cannot be handled in mathematical terms are then of little interest. Other neoclassical economists may recall that Joseph Schumpeter has written extensively on innovation, 'creative destruction' and technological progress more generally (Schumpeter, 1942), but would then perhaps recommend a department of economic history as the right place for studies of this kind.

A third line of reasoning might be to argue that decision trees are used in game theory, and there is nothing new with decision trees for the neoclassical economist. It is true that decision trees are common in game theory but then one has to make distinctions between different kinds of decision trees. In game theory of the conventional kind, the analysis is, as I see it, mechanical with one-dimensional quantitative 'pay-offs' at the end of each branch in the decision tree to make mathematical treatment possible. The results (pay-offs) follow from the assumptions that you feed into the process at the very beginning.

Our decision tree is more 'open-ended' and normally refers to a 'never-ending' process. There are no one-dimensional quantitative pay-offs but only a series of (monetary and non-monetary) outcomes for each period and a series of incompletely known positions that may be understood in qualitative, quantitative and visual terms.[3]

Example 2: Land-use planning

My early study of inertia and irreversibility in relation to R&D was later followed by a more general study of inertia in all kinds of non-monetary dimensions (Söderbaum, 1973). Issues of environment and natural resources then come to the forefront. In many countries, people are moving from the countryside to the cities. Urbanization is one of the phenomena of globalization. Space is needed for dwelling, offices, streets, roads, etc.

This may sound like a natural phenomenon and one we should not worry much about. One might argue that people need somewhere to live and for this purpose house construction is necessary. Roads and streets are also needed. But in specific regions and globally, large amounts of agricultural land and forests are transformed for urbanization and transportation purposes. Expansion of space for these purposes aggravates existing CO_2 problems and forecloses the use of agricultural land for food production at future points in time and the use of forests as a renewable resource. House construction and road building are essentially irreversible processes. It is not easy to return to the previous position if one wishes to do so.

For a certain plot of agricultural land, the options at t_0 are assumed to be 'continued use as agricultural land', a transfer to agro-forestry or to asphalt (connected with road construction). In the case of agro-forestry, there is a possibility later to return to agricultural land, if desired at that time (see Figure 7.2). There is no arrow back to agricultural land from 'asphalt' suggesting that this is an irreversible change. Politicians or other decision-makers may in specific cases, accept such impacts. As a minimum, such consequences should be illuminated so that decision-makers know what they are doing and can consider their responsibilities.

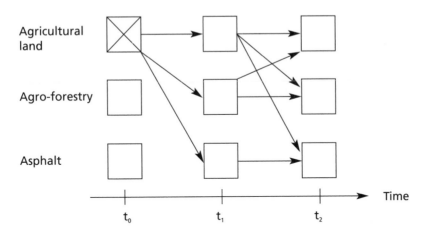

Figure 7.2 *Decision tree applied to land-use planning. Options at different points in time can be illustrated or 'illuminated' for decision-makers and other concerned actors*

In the Västra Nåntuna case described earlier (Chapter 2), politicians act as if they do not want to know what they are doing and those employed in the municipality and county administration behave as if their task is to facilitate implementation of the house-construction alternative and nothing else. They are giving little concern to environmental and sustainability issues.

Example 3: Construction of dams in developing countries

In countries such as the US, Sweden and other European countries, many big and small dams have been built for the production of electricity and other purposes. Rivers and connected ecosystems have been transformed, and fisheries and tourist interests have suffered. In Sweden, this process has essentially been stopped but Swedish construction companies see new opportunities in the form of partnerships with actors in developing countries.

These are also examples of processes that are essentially irreversible. This means that there are many reasons to think before acting. Irreversibility and other impacts upon future options should be illuminated rather than darkened. One important development is that CBA has become increasingly questioned as a way of preparing investments in dams. The World Commission on Dams (WCD, 2000) instead recommends MCAs to preparing decisions since these approaches are more transparent and open.

The members of the WCD represent various stakeholder categories, including national governments, construction companies and indigenous people. When building large dams in developing countries (and even in so-called developed countries), indigenous people living close to the river are often one of the groups that suffer the most, making resettlement an issue. The WCD report (2000) made it clear that resettlement of indigenous people is an ethical issue that cannot be solved by CBA calculation. Indigenous people are dependent upon the socio-cultural and ecological context. Neither can monetary compensation solve the ethical dilemma. And even for individuals and organizations that do not belong to the indigenous category, ethical and ideological issues cannot be escaped.

A classification of approaches

Four categories of approaches to decision-making can be identified (see Table 7.2). Such approaches can be aggregated or disaggregated, they can be ethically/ideologically closed or open. For example, CBA fits nicely into the highly aggregated/ideologically closed category 'a'. All impacts are reduced to their alleged monetary equivalent (i.e. 'monetary reductionism') based on the neoclassical market ideology of 'correct values' for purposes of societal resource allocation. To be more precise, reference can be made to three kinds of reductionism:

- multidimensional impacts are reduced to one-dimensional monetary impacts;
- impacts affecting different groups of individuals, organizations and interests are reduced to one-dimensional monetary impacts;

- impacts expected for different future periods and points in time are reduced to one point in time (as a present value).

This way of reducing different types of impacts for each alternative to one number in monetary terms is heroic, to say the least. It can only be accomplished by a kind of ethical or ideological reductionism. All possible ethical or ideological orientations are reduced to one ethics or ideology. The CBA model is ethically or 'ideologically closed', to use the terminology in Table 7.2. The CBA idea of valuation is furthermore much more precise than any of the established political ideologies such as social democracy or liberalism. And it is advocated in the name of science.

Table 7.2 *A classification of approaches to decision-making and evaluation*

	Ideologically closed	Ideologically open
Highly aggregated	a	b
Highly disaggregated	c	d

Source: Söderbaum, 2000, p80

Table 7.2 also suggests where to look for alternatives to CBA. Among such alternatives, PA belongs to category 'd', i.e. disaggregated and ideologically open approaches. As has already been argued CBA is far from being compatible with SD, while PA implies openings for SD and in that sense is closer to SD. As interpreted in previous chapters, SD:

- is multidimensional in its way of dealing with non-monetary impacts that are specific in their logic (path-dependence, inertia and often irreversibility) when compared with monetary impacts; the meaning of non-degradation of the natural resource base, now and in the future, should be articulated in relation to each decision situation;
- relies heavily on the precautionary principle, prevention rather than cure;
- is ethically/ideologically open referring to competing ideological orientations rather than dictating one ethics (ideology) as correct;
- points to democracy as a guiding principle for the analyst in relation to politicians, stakeholders and other actors and more generally for the search and decision process; listening to many voices concerning how the problem is understood, identification of alternatives and possibly relevant ideological orientations are parts of this ambition to strengthen (rather than weaken) democracy.

One of the ideas behind PA is to study the alternatives considered with an equal ambition concerning search for impacts, etc. Since PA is not the only alternative to CBA, one may argue that other methods, such as EIA (Glasson et al, 1994), strategic environmental assessment (Dalal-Clayton and Sadler, 2005), social impact assessment, health impact assessment and MCAs should also be carefully described and considered. For reasons of space (and vested interests in PA, one should add), this will not be done here. I only discuss EIA and MCAs. The purpose is to point to my understanding of their strengths and weaknesses.[4]

Environmental impact assessment

When compared with CBA, EIA is a relatively recent phenomenon. Its history goes back to the early 1970s and the National Environmental Policy Act (NEPA) in the US. This was a period when environmental problems were taken seriously in many countries. Interest in these issues grew following the book *Silent Spring* by Rachel Carson (1962), writings by other authors and initiatives such as the already mentioned Stockholm conference. There was considerable social pressure from some scientists and the public to do something.

While EIA (like PA) essentially belongs to category 'd' in Table 7.2, EIA is a complementary and 'partial' approach rather than a 'total' approach, the latter attempting to cover all kinds of impacts. When the NEPA was introduced, it was argued that technical and financial issues were normally well covered as a basis for investments in infrastructure (dams, motorways, airports, etc.) while environmental impacts played a peripheral role. A complementary approach was needed. EIA should be carried out by the agency or company responsible for the proposed investment in cases where there are 'significant environmental impacts'. Such impacts should be described in detail, also covering matters such as biodiversity loss, when relevant. In this way, together with other methods used, a more balanced view of the pros and cons of a project should be obtained.

Following the early US initiative, EIA has become institutionalized in laws and directives in many parts of the world. A number of textbooks about EIA exist. While PA and MCA (see below) are largely limited to university research so far, EIA is part of practical policy implementation. In the EU, there are directives for environmental assessment (EU Directive 2001/42/EC) that should be respected in member countries. In general terms, EIA can be said to cover the following items:

- the expected environmental impacts (in a rather broad sense) of a proposed project, programme or policy;

- a special focus on irreversible impacts or impacts that cannot easily be reversed;
- alternatives to the proposed project (programme, policy) should be identified and evaluated (could the same objective be attained with some alternative project while avoiding some of the negative environmental impacts?);
- consideration of possibilities to modify the project to avoid some of the negative environmental impacts (so-called 'mitigating measures').

The existence of EIA recommendations and laws in many countries is certainly influential. Actors who take environmental issues seriously can refer to the need and obligation to carry out an EIA and point to items that should be covered. EIA is a highly disaggregated approach in the sense that the different types of environmental impacts are considered separately. EIA points to the importance of environmental impacts but is otherwise relatively open in ethical-ideological terms.

The partial nature of EIA is at the same time its strength and a weakness. If actors in decision-making positions make the judgement that there are 'no significant environmental impacts' connected with the project and no other actor challenges this statement, no EIA will be carried out. Another weakness of this approach has to do with the fact that it is the relevant governmental agency or construction company proposing the project that is initiating the EIA study and thereby to some extent is controlling its content. If the initiating agency or corporation is strongly committed to the proposed alternative, the EIA study may be manipulated to reflect this. EIA studies are often carried out by consulting companies who may be eager to behave in a way that facilitates future orders.

EIA deals largely with natural science impacts. The social science and democracy aspects are not always well handled. Is it possible for all stakeholders and other concerned actors to participate in the process of carrying out an EIA? Is the process open to the public or does it rather fall under the technocratic and closed category 'c' in Table 7.2? In conclusion, there are weaknesses with EIA but the existence of this institution can still be an important step towards SD. The bigger issue is whether further steps can be taken in the same direction.

Multi-criteria approaches

Another alternative (or set of alternatives) to CBA is MCAs. Contrary to CBA, which relies heavily on one (monetary) criterion, a move in the multidimensional and multi-criteria direction is suggested to allow for some complexity rather than assume it away. One difficulty in describing and commenting upon

MCAs is that there are many (competing) MCAs rather than one. This diversity of approaches concerns the technicalities of any single approach and how politicians, stakeholders (interested parties) and other actors are involved.[5]

There is a kind of democratic ambition behind single MCAs. One way of dealing with differences in decision-makers' value orientation is to attempt to identify one (one-dimensional) objective function for each decision-maker and then construct a ranking from the point of view of each decision-maker. A different line of reasoning is to organize arenas where citizens can meet for a dialogue and for attempts to get closer to each other in terms of ideological orientation (to use our language), preferences for alternatives and solutions to the problems faced. Theories about a dialogic approach and about engagement are relevant here (Bebbington et al, 2007b), as are practical efforts referred to as citizen's juries (Coote and Lenaghan, 1997).

Efforts to involve citizens, stakeholders and other concerned actors in a dialogue as part of the problem-solving process are generally welcome and we can learn from such experiments and experiences. But such efforts should be complementary to, rather than replace, studies carried out by the local or national administration. Responsibility should finally reside with the democratically elected politicians. Accountability has to be taken seriously (Lewin, 2007). For this reason more technically oriented studies carried out by an analyst should be used in combination with various attempts to involve stakeholders and other actors. And the two processes should mutually support each other.

The idea of presenting a multiplicity of approaches for choice in each decision situation inherent in MCAs may sound attractive. However, moving back and forth between approaches can also be a source of confusion. There has to be some stability in terms of the rules of the game for preparing decisions and involving stakeholders and citizens. Accountability is made much more difficult in the absence of stability.

Advocacy for MCAs is a relatively recent phenomenon and this category of approaches is at an early stage of being implemented and institutionalized. It is interesting to note, however, that the WCD (2000) points in this direction by elaborating one specific version of an MCA in its recommendations. However, the WCD does not go directly to a technical analysis of alternatives and impacts. Instead, they start by discussing a 'Normative Development Framework' in the sense of the Universal Declaration of Human Rights, The United Nations Declaration on the Right to Development and the Rio Declaration on Environment and Development. This is followed by a set of 'core values' proposed by WCD namely 'Equity, Efficiency, Participatory Decision-Making, Sustainability, Accountability' (WCD, 2000, p202). This in turn leads to 'A set of Guidelines for Good Practice' subdivided into seven 'strategic priorities' (p278). The first priority is about stakeholder analysis and

'Gaining Public Acceptance' and the second strategic priority describes a number of tools for 'Comprehensive Options Assessment'. 'Strategic Impact Assessment' is suggested for 'Environmental, Social, Health and Cultural Heritage Issues' and at the project level MCAs are one among many possibilities.

MCA processes, as described by WCD, use a mix of qualitative and quantitative criteria to assess and compare options. 'Stakeholder-driven MCA processes are flexible and open, based on the concept of stakeholder forum' (WCD, 2000, p285) It is argued that the MCA process 'cannot resolve all conflicts' but may 'assist in identifying policy scenarios and the way different groups and interests perceive them' (WCD, 2000, p285).

The purpose of PA as previously described is to 'illuminate' an issue and something similar holds for the WCD approach to decision-making. As part of PA, reference is made to ideology and ideological orientation and it is clear that the WCD (while not using the term 'ideology') points in a similar direction by referring to human rights and SD. Participation, accountability and other aspects of democracy are regarded as essential to public acceptance and progress.

Positional analysis as a sustainability assessment model

As previously noted, PA is part of institutional economics. The purpose is to 'illuminate' an issue or decision situation in a many-sided way to actors and decision-makers who normally differ with respect to how they are positioned in relation to the issue and their ideological orientation. More precisely in relation to a decision situation the PA study should be used to 'illuminate':

- Ethical/ideological issues that appear relevant to citizens, stakeholders and decision-makers such as politicians – this can be done by articulating competing ideological orientations.
- Alternatives of choice that appear relevant in relation to the ideological orientations articulated – for reasons of intelligibility the main alternatives considered should be limited to three or four.
- Non-monetary and monetary impacts of each alternative in a largely disaggregated way in relation to time and affected groups of individuals or organizations – special focus should be on uncertainties concerning the feasibility of specific alternatives and on impacts that are irreversible or difficult to reverse;
- Conflicts of interest – this can be done by identifying activities of individuals (organizations) that will be differently affected depending on which alternative is chosen.

The ambition is to make a study that strengthens democracy and reduces manipulation. As many persons as possible should find the analysis useful for understanding the issue faced and recognizing that their interests are somehow visible in the study. The study is also designed to be compatible with various attempts to engage citizens, stakeholders and other actors in an open dialogue in available arenas (and perhaps arenas constructed for the purpose of dialogue and problem-solving concerning the specific issue at hand).

This 'democracy orientation' goes against the 'technocracy orientation' previously discussed where clear-cut solutions and a different kind of expertise are expected. Some technocrats even argue that the term 'method' should be limited to cases where the analyst is able to refer to alleged common values and rank the alternatives considered accordingly.

Essential components of a PA study are (c.f., Söderbaum, 2000, pp89–100, 2006, 2007a):

- PEP and PEO assumptions;
- historical background of the issue (Are there previous studies or documents?);
- dialogue between analyst, stakeholders and concerned actors about how problems are perceived and how to deal with the problems in a process of interactive learning;
- identification and development of relevant ideological orientations;
- many-sided search for alternatives that match the diversity of ideological orientations;
- equal treatment of alternatives considered;
- a multidimensional and ideologically open idea of economics and efficiency;
- systems thinking as a way of identifying impacts of various kinds (What kind of systems will be affected differently depending on which one of the alternatives that is chosen? What is the spatial extension of these systems? How does the specific decision situation relate to broader policy issues, for example at the national level?);
- systematic focus on how non-monetary and monetary impacts differ between alternatives;
- positional thinking as a way of considering inertia (for example path-dependence, irreversibility) and more generally impacts on future options by choosing one alternative rather than another;
- attempts to systematically deal with uncertainty in terms of scenarios and in other ways;
- systematic comparison of alternatives with respect to impacts of different kinds and in relation to various groups of stakeholders;
- analysis of commonalities and conflicts of interest in relation to various affected activities (of individuals and organizations);

- conditional conclusions of analysis in relation to possibly relevant ideological orientations to be presented to decision-makers, stakeholders and other actors;
- an idea of decision-making as a 'matching' or 'pattern-recognition' process (see Figure 4.2);
- feedback from all actors, ideally at all stages of analysis and improvements of information base for decisions;
- an indicator framework for the monitoring of impacts and *ex post* evaluation (follow-up studies).

One idea behind PA is that the analyst should take different kinds of ideological orientations seriously. A pure monetary profits and economic growth ideology should not be excluded if there are actors and political parties that seriously refer to such an ideology. Our main interest here is, however, SD therefore sustainability assessment. For PA to qualify as a sustainability assessment model (SAM) at least one of the ideological orientations articulated and used for evaluation and ranking of alternatives should refer to a specific interpretation of SD (Brown and Frame, 2005; Bebbington et al, 2007a; Söderbaum, 2007a).

Applied studies with positional analysis

PA as an approach to decision-making was originally presented in Swedish, and applied studies have therefore mainly been published in the Swedish, Norwegian and Finnish languages. Many of these studies are Master theses by students but also five PhD studies in the fields of forestry, energy systems, water management and transportation can be reported. In English the theoretical background and principles of PA has been presented in books and articles (for example Söderbaum, 1982b, 2000, 2006, 2007a). These presentations have only in exceptional cases provided sufficient guidance for applied studies written in English (Mafunda and Navrud, 1995; Attwater, 1996). Ralph Hall's (2006) PhD thesis *Understanding and Applying the Concept of Sustainable Development to Transportation Planning and Decision-Making in the US* at MIT, Boston, is a recent study. Hall attempted to combine elements from two largely compatible approaches, Nicholas Ashford's trade-off analysis (see for example Ashford, 1981) and PA.

For PA to be seriously considered in the English-speaking world, both textbooks and applied studies are probably needed. To become useful, an approach need, however, not necessarily be applied in detail. As in the case of Ralph Hall (2006), ideas from PA can be combined with elements from other approaches to form 'mixed' approaches. PA can also be regarded as one among the MCAs or as part of a systems approach to sustainability (Clayton and Radcliffe, 1996, pp190–194).

A number of alternatives or complements to CBA have been proposed over the years and it is clear that CBA is losing ground among approaches to decision-making. There are still actors who 'demand' CBA and not only among neoclassical economists with their vested interests. Many politicians and civil servants do not know of any other approach.

In society, specific expectations on scientists and experts have been institutionalized over the years. An expert advising politicians should come up with clear-cut solutions, it is believed. The analyst should be able to rank the alternatives and be able to identify the 'best' option from a societal point of view. It is then possible for politicians to hide behind this expert judgement. Responsibility is shared with the expert or in the extreme case, shifted to the expert. This way of looking upon decision-making is very different from the story told in this book. Instead of relying on 'experts in correct valuation tools and values' and thereby transforming complexity to simplicity, it is argued that complexity should be accepted and handled at least in part.

Problems (and connected complexity) in relation to decision-making and sustainability assessment are of many kinds:

- In a democracy one has to accept (and indeed welcome) the existence of more than one basis for valuation or ideological orientation. Even for one individual the task of relating intrinsic values to those that are more exchangeable may be very difficult.
- Information about the ideological orientation of different interested parties, information about alternatives and about impacts for given alternatives is normally limited and fragmented suggesting that considerable uncertainty is involved.
- Irreversibility in non-monetary terms is a normal phenomenon in relation to sustainability issues. When combined with the existence of intrinsic values (in the eyes of some actors or interested parties), it becomes clear that making a decision is not always a simple matter.

This means that one has to live with complexity and that this complexity should be handled and made explicit in the analysis carried out. The task is one of systematically searching for relevant information to illuminate an issue. This goes against the popular idea that every problem has a solution. In a jigsaw puzzle, the pieces fit together only in one way; in mathematics, the tendency is similarly to refer to one correct solution. And, as already alluded to, many economists probably hesitate to use the word 'method' about an approach that after systematic analysis ends with conditional conclusions.

Among ecological economists, Silvio Funtowicz, Jerome Ravetz and

Martin O'Connor have repeatedly pointed to the need to deal with complexity and referred to sustainability issues as 'messy' or 'wicked' when compared with traditional problem-solving (Funtowicz and Ravetz, 1991, 1994; Funtowicz et al, 1998; see also Frame and Brown, 2008). They point to uncertainty, irreversibility and valuation as aspects of complexity and argue that 'normal science' in the sense of paradigm and paradigm shift (Kuhn, 1970) becomes less relevant. A 'post-normal' view of science is needed where the roles of scientists and laypersons change considerably. Expertise should be democratized and laypersons (interested parties and other actors) increasingly involved in decision processes for their specific competencies and because of the rights in a democracy to participate. This suggests a need for 'extended peer communities'. Analysts need to listen to many voices and learn by interacting with interested parties and other actors.

These arguments point in the direction of moving away from 'ideologically closed', 'highly aggregated' approaches to those that are ideologically open and disaggregated (see Table 7.2). A significant move away from technocracy in the direction of democracy is needed and the analyst – while still working systematically and respecting many traditional imperatives of good science – has to become a more humble person.

Follow-up studies of projects, programmes and policies

The term sustainability assessment may as well be used both in preparing decisions and follow-up studies. It can be argued here that PA is also useful to follow up decisions made concerning the implementation of specific projects, programmes or policies. Standardized monitoring systems can be used for this purpose, so can a set of *ad hoc* indicators tailor-made for the project (programme, policy).

The distinction between monetary and non-monetary impacts and between flows and positions is as relevant for *ex post* (follow-up) studies as for preparing decisions (*ex ante* studies). Thinking in multiple-step positional terms considering irreversibility, etc. is no less relevant while studying actual impacts of a project and how it opens and closes options for future points and periods of time.

The fact that one alternative was chosen over another (among the previously considered alternatives) does not make it less relevant to compare alternatives after implementation of a project. Actual outcomes can be compared with the hypothetical case that some other of the previously considered alternatives had been chosen. Continuing as before – a so-called zero alternative or 'do nothing' option – is often a relevant alternative for such systematic comparison.

The issue of competing ideological orientations is similarly as relevant when evaluating the outcomes of a project. In a democracy one cannot assume that all citizens, stakeholders and other actors agree about an ideological direction. Some actors may regard a project as very successful in relation to their ideology and interests (pure monetary profits and economic growth, for instance) while others look upon the project as a step in the wrong direction (for example strengthening unsustainable trends).

Listening to the stories told by various stakeholders and actors is as important in *ex post* as in *ex ante* studies. Are the actors who advocated the project happy with the outcomes or disappointed in some respects? What are the stories told by people who questioned the project from the very beginning and at that time advocated some other option. We are back to the imperative to live with some complexity and respect each other even when ideas about a desirable future differ. Carrying out preparatory studies and follow-up studies is thought of as a way of learning and strengthening the accountability of actors in responsible positions. Avoiding dialogue and studies will rather create tensions between various stakeholders and political groups in society and is in this sense a dangerous strategy.

The experience of applying PA for *ex post* purposes, so-called 'retrospective PA', is limited. In one case, Kil, a municipality in Sweden, decided in the 1970s to invest in bio-energy and change its urban heat system to pellets from oil. A follow-up study was made in the early 1990s where the outcome of the actual investment was compared to the hypothetical case that Kil had continued with its fossil fuel-based system during the period. It was concluded that the energy system with pellets did not cost more in monetary terms and represented an improvement in terms of impacts upon local employment and emissions of CO_2 (Forsberg, 1993). In a second case, the conceptual framework of PA was used in historically recapitulating the decision process and its impacts concerning a dam and hydro power plant, Urrá I, which was built in Columbia (Edlund and Quintero, 1995).

Notes

1   It should be added that CBA belongs to the weaker parts of neoclassical economics. Some other parts cannot be dismissed so easily.
2   Other elements of PA will be presented later in a scheme of analysis.
3   Oscar Morgenstern, regarded by many as one of the fathers of game theory, read my PhD study *Positionsanalys vid beslutsfattande och planering* (Söderbaum, 1973) and made the comment that decision-making is more complex than usually assumed: 'Your book is another illustration of how difficult it is to analyse what correct decisions are. That was once thought to be a very simple matter, but as so often happens in scientific development, things turned out to be far more compli-

cated than one ever imagined.' With his German background and familiarity with the writings of Swedish economists in the 1930s and 1940s, Morgenstern was able to read texts in Swedish. He was, at the time, connected with Mathematica Inc., Princeton, New Jersey (Letter to the author 15 July 1975).

4   A more ambitious attempt to compare different methods is available in Söderbaum (2004c).

5   This means that even PA can be seen as being part of the broad MCA category.

Further readings

CBA of the monetary kind is an approach to decision-making and in spite of its many weaknesses, it tends to survive. Many have become accustomed to think of values in monetary terms and to expect clear-cut answers from analysts as experts. The debate continues, however, and Frank Ackerman and Lisa Heinzerling are among the critics in their book *Priceless. On Knowing the Price of Everything and the Value of Nothing* (2004) while Cass Sunstein tends to defend CBA in his book *Risk and Reason. Safety, Law and the Environment* (2002).

Questions for discussion

➤ In this book it has been argued that 'monetary reductionism' is part of the problem rather than any solution. Science cannot dictate correct values or rules of evaluation. We live in democratic societies and therefore ought to carry out an analysis with openings for more than one ideological orientation. This points to methods where complexity is accepted rather than assumed away. What is your opinion about the alternatives to CBA presented?

➤ Think of a decision situation in your private life and try to apply some of the steps in positional analysis. Try then as a second step to follow the same procedure concerning a decision situation at the societal level. Do you think that this way of systematically preparing decisions is meaningful in relation to SD?

8

Towards Sustainability Economics

A number of unsustainable trends have been discussed in this book and others can easily be added. Fish stocks have been depleted in many parts of the world, surface and subsoil water is contaminated because of lack of sanitation, and pollution from agriculture, industry and from transportation activities continues to increase with their emissions of CO_2, particles and other substances. There is a current boom in mining activities and stocks of radioactive and other hazardous waste tend to accumulate. Urban space is increasing in many parts of the world while space for forests, agriculture and non-human species is being reduced. Biodiversity loss is reported for different ecosystems.

Other elements of SD such as health, poverty, equality, human rights and protection of cultural artefacts are not performing much better. In the name of 'progress' through 'globalization' or 'market expansion', the degradation of ecosystems and the natural resource base continues. Some ruling business elites may be content with this development pattern while a large proportion of the global population suffers.

Although some of these problems have become aggravated, many of them were known at the time of the Stockholm Conference on the Human Environment in 1972. It is also true that awareness about the existence of serious problems has increased in many circles. But there is also a paralysis and inability to act in too many cases. Actors in powerful positions often deny or downplay the problems or shift responsibility to others. They may even believe that continued economic growth will, in some mysterious way, solve the problems.

Why is this the case? I have argued that it is not enough to focus directly on each specific environmental issue. There is a choice and there are alternatives as well at a more fundamental level – the level of perspectives. Ideas about good science, paradigms in economics and ideological orientations have to be scrutinized. Power relationships and institutional arrangements tend to follow from the choices made in terms of the mentioned perspectives. And when an increasing number of actors shift from one perspective or orientation to another, problems will be perceived in new ways and action will hopefully follow.

Nobody can claim to have the final answers to the issues raised but each actor can present her or his beliefs and experiences. My judgements are those of an economist who is not part of the mainstream among economists but who, by contrast, may be part of a mainstream in society more generally or in the social sciences.

There are alternatives to neoclassical economics

Mainstream neoclassical economists claim to provide us with a conceptual framework and ideas about 'efficient resource allocation'. However, doubts about the appropriateness of these recommendations are increasing in many circles and some point to a crisis in economics and a related crisis in development thinking (for example Fullbrook, 2003). One mistake by neoclassical economists is to claim that their conceptual framework is useful and the best for all purposes or fields of enquiry. In this book I have tried to show that a different conceptual framework is needed for issues related to sustainability and development in a broad sense.

A typical neoclassical economist would argue that there are no alternatives to the neoclassical theoretical perspective. Again, this is a subject that I have tried to cover by articulating one alternative among others to neoclassical thinking and advice. Some features of this alternative economics can be described as follows:

- Economics is always political economics. The idea of value neutrality is abandoned. Neoclassical economics (as well as alternative perspectives) has a special ideological content. There is a choice between different kinds of 'political economics'.
- If economics is political economics, then normal imperatives of democracy have to be observed in economic science and practice.
- Individuals and organizations are actors related to a social, institutional, ecological and political context. The context can also be divided into a market and non-market part.
- Individuals and organizations are socially embedded in the economy and the individual, organization and the economy are embedded in the ecosphere.
- No rigid assumptions are made about the objectives or ideological orientation of individuals and mission statements of organizations. Notwithstanding inertia and path-dependence, ideological orientation and mission statement are subject to reconsideration and do change over time.
- Monetary analysis is only partial analysis. A multidimensional perspective is suggested where the logic differs between the monetary and non-monetary side. Inertia, path-dependence and irreversibility are characteristics particularly on the non-monetary side.
- Decision-making is understood as a matching process where ideological

orientation and expected impact profile of specific alternatives are confronted.

- Efficiency in the management of resources is largely an open issue and related to the ideological orientation of the observer, assessing either activities at the micro level or the economy as a whole.
- Institutional change processes are understood in terms of how actors interpret specific phenomena, how these phenomena are named and otherwise manifested in language, conceptual models, organization and become legitimate or not in a larger population of actors.

This institutional version of political economics has been described at length in the previous chapters and will not be further elaborated here.

Neo-liberalism as understood by civil society intellectuals

In her thoughtful book *The Blockage*, Eva Kras (2007) argues that many influential actors understand that society faces a number of complex problems, but that the same actors still experience difficulties in changing their thinking and behaviour. 'Our "business-as-usual" values have prevailed as unquestioned truths' (Kras, 2007, p2). This inability to seriously question established thought patterns is referred to as 'blockage'. According to Kras, one way of dealing with this is to listen to a number of 'visionaries', i.e. persons that focus on our 'deeply held values' and how they can guide us. Previously mentioned civil society intellectuals such as Vandana Shiva and David Korten belong to this category of visionaries but there are many others.

As part of traditional positivistic ideas of science and even so-called 'sustainability science' (Kates et al, 2001; Clark and Dickson, 2003), the tendency has been to leave issues of vision and ideology to politicians. Contrary to this division of labour, Eva Kras (2007) argues that if the problems faced are problems of ideology and vision, then it is a mistake to exclude this aspect from consideration and analysis. As scholars, we should instead participate in a dialogue with politicians and other actors about interpretations of sustainability and visions of a sustainable society as well as competing visions, such as the one connected with neo-liberalism. There is a need for creative thinking also in this area.

Today, a large number of actors in business and politics embrace the beliefs of neo-liberalism that, according to the present author, are not conducive to sustainability. One international group of leading civil society intellectuals suggests the following list of key features of 'economic globalization – sometimes referred to as corporate globalization or neo-liberalism' (International Forum on Globalization, 2002, p19):

- promotion of hypergrowth and unrestricted exploitation of environmental resources to fuel that growth;
- privatization and commodification of public services and of remaining aspects of the global and community commons;
- global cultural and economic homogenization and the intense promotion of consumerism;
- integration and conversion of national economies, including some that were largely self-reliant, to environmentally and socially harmful export-oriented production;
- corporate deregulation and unrestricted movement of capital across borders;
- dramatically increased corporate concentration;
- dismantling of public health, social and environmental programmes already in place;
- replacement of traditional powers of democratic nation states and local communities by global corporate bureaucracies.

This is not a kind description of neo-liberalism but it is certainly correct for the civil society intellectuals who are co-authors of the book cited. Neo-liberalism is also connected with the so-called Washington Consensus, i.e. an alleged agreement about a certain ideology and policy package by international institutions located in Washington DC, especially the World Bank and the International Monetary Fund (IMF). The person who coined 'Washington Consensus' as a term is John Williamson and his list of characteristics overlaps in many ways with the above list, for instance by pointing to 'trade liberalization, liberalization of inflows of foreign direct investment, privatization, deregulation (to abolish barriers to entry and exit), secure property rights' (Williamson, 1990, pp252–53). Williamson later commented upon how the concept of Washington Consensus has been understood and used by different actor groups. He also tried to explain what he originally meant and his present thinking based on the debate that has followed (Williamson, 2000).

The combined impact of neoclassical economics and neo-liberalism

According to our earlier model of 'drivers' of institutional change processes, it is not enough to point to the dominant paradigm in economics to understand institutional change processes. What matters is the combination of dominant theory of science, dominant paradigm and dominant ideological orientation. Neo-liberals seldom declare openly that they believe in neoclassical economics or that neo-liberalism is largely based upon the neoclassical conceptual framework. Susan George, one of the visionaries that we should listen to, does not even make a distinction between neoclassical economics and neo-liberalism by referring to 'neo-liberal economics' (George, 2007, personal communication). One leading civil society intellectual, Nicanor Perlas at the Center for Alternative Development Initiatives (CADI) institute, The Philippines, uses the same terminology (Perlas, 2000) while Alexander Gillespie (2001, p36) suggests 'neo-economic liberalism'. The labels 'neo-liberal economics' and 'neo-economic liberalism' certainly have their advantages. Neo-liberalism is a kind of market fundamentalism but neoclassical economists need not espouse all the aspects of this fundamentalism.

Let us first look at the ideological similarities between neoclassical economics and neo-liberalism:

- There is a focus on markets in both cases and concerns outside the market receive only scarce attention.
- Economic growth in GDP terms is the main indicator of progress in society.
- The only organization seriously considered is the firm or business corporation.
- The consumer is the king and the consumer is supposed to consider only short-run utility rather than bother about what is now referred to as sustainability (impacts upon others, future generations, society at large). In both cases we are dealing with an ideology of 'consumerism'.
- When dealing with markets and international trade, the focus is narrow in both cases in the sense of referring to one commodity at a time. Reasoning in terms of multiple transactions, multiple interests, multifunctionality is avoided.
- Analysis is largely monetary in kind as in the case of CBA. Even 'neoclassical environmental economics' emphasizes markets and the monetary dimension.
- The efficiency idea is the same in both cases, referring to the monetary cost of each unit produced, sold or bought.
- The simplistic nature of international trade theory means that this theory supports export-oriented production at the expense of local or regional self-reliance.
- Neoclassical economists similarly tend to believe that unrestricted capital movement across borders is good for efficiency in a global perspective.

But neoclassical economics need not be as repugnant as neo-liberalism in some other respects:

- While neoclassical analysis is of little help in opening the door for alternative ideas about efficiency, neoclassical economists are not necessarily in favour of privatization of common property.

- While being silent about power issues, neoclassical economists need not support the uncontrolled growth of business corporations. They often argue that competition is more efficient than monopolies and cartels.
- Among neoclassical economists many are social democrats (at least in Sweden) that are in favour of a state with considerable regulatory powers.

While there is no complete identity, this comparison suggests that neoclassical theory conceptually and ideologically in many ways legitimizes neo-liberalism. It should always be remembered that thousands and thousands of students all over the world are indoctrinated in the belief system of neoclassical economics every year. Together with the activities of large business corporations, media and neo-liberal think-tanks, the dominance of a market ideology in current society is not unexpected. Many professionals and political leaders do not know of any other economics.

In 2001, a group of scholars in the Czech Republic initiated a dialogue with the question *Is Globalization Overpowering Democracy?* (Lapka et al, 2007). The kind of globalization challenged is globalization of markets and the right of private business to penetrate every corner of the world. The question asked is whether there is a conflict between globalization of markets, so-called 'corporate globalization', and democracy. Democracy is a sensitive issue for many of us and perhaps more so in countries that have left the Soviet system behind. Are these countries (to use market language) simply 'exchanging' one kind of dictatorship (or one system with limited democracy) for another? Is the market always an instrument for democracy or does it sometimes work against it and reduce the role of democracy?

Sweden is still a country with a mixed economy, but recently with the new right–centre government, privatization is no longer an excluded option. In Täby, a municipality close to Stockholm, leading right-wing politicians (in Swedish: '*moderater*') recently wished to privatize the Tibble gymnasium. The principal at the time (and one or two additional persons) wished to become the new owner of the school. A majority of teachers and students were against the idea and suggested a voting procedure but this proposal was dismissed as irrelevant by the rector and a right-wing majority in the local government. Those who wish to vote can do so but it does not change anything.

This case suggests that if there is a private actor ready to take over and transform common property to private property, then this is seen as a step forward by neo-liberals. No study of expected monetary and non-monetary impacts for taxpayers and other interested parties was needed. The case suggests a serious contradiction between neo-liberalism and democracy. Neo-liberalism as fundamentalism may be as dangerous as other kinds of fundamentalism. For some actors, the right to gain privately by transfer of property from common to private appears to stand above democracy. One may ask whether neo-liberals in their emphasis on individualism are able to perceive any common values at all.

Unsustainable trends and path-dependence

We are faced with a number of unsustainable trends from the local to the global and also with inertia and path-dependence. How can we go about changing the direction of those unsustainable trends with a hope of approaching a sustainable society?

Path-dependence was discussed in relation to Figure 7.1. A trend can be described in many ways. In this case it is considered as a series of positions from one point in time to the next. The stock of a certain species of fish is reduced in a water ecosystem or urban space is increased in absolute and relative terms in the municipality of Uppsala (or in the EU). The logic connected with decision trees can be a starting point for illustrating the mentioned trends, with time indicated on the horizontal axis and the stock of a certain fish species on the vertical axis. The vertical axis may alternatively indicate the total number of hectares used for urban space (including housing, roads, offices, supermarkets, etc.). Present and future options, irreversibility included, can be illustrated, as in Figure 7.2. We need these diagrams to realize what we are doing in non-monetary terms.

Inertia and path-dependence interpreted in positional terms may also refer to an actor's ideas about good science, about paradigms in economics or ideological orientation in a broader sense. Thus, we are facing a lot of inertia or 'blockage', to use the words of Eva Kras (2007) once more. Ideological orientation is part of an actor's identity and therefore one has to tread cautiously.

Through advertising and propaganda of the neoclassical and neo-liberal kind we have all become good consumers contributing actively to the monetary profits of business corporations and to the growth of the economy in monetary terms. A large number of institutions have been formed and adapted to facilitate economic growth, increased incomes and wealth accumulation. How can all this be turned around to enter a more sustainable path?

I have no easy answer to this except by pointing to the need for a dialogue about perspectives of the kinds mentioned and to listen to visionaries. Buzzwords, such as 'sustainability' play a role in this. My students have told me about the King of Thailand, Bhumibol Adulyadej, Rama IX, who uses the words 'sufficiency economy' as his vision. What is the meaning of such a sufficiency economy and how can we get there? The United Nations Development Programme (UNDP) has followed up this issue (UNDP, 2007). The economy of Thailand was for a period among the 'tiger economies' with exceptionally high growth rates in GDP terms. While growth was high, inequality within the country became more accentuated and the export-oriented economy was vulnerable to external shocks. The crisis in this part of the world in 1997 led to a questioning of the focus on economic growth and exports. A more robust economy with community building and local self-reliance as some of the imperatives became the alternative. 'Natural resources are key foundation for self-reliance. Sufficiency thinking has evolved several techniques for non-intrusive, sustainable approaches to conserving the natural environment' (UNDP, 2007, pxvii). A people-centred approach to development with emphasis on education, health and philosophical and spiritual issues became the alternative. Non-monetary objectives such as those of the MDGs were upgraded: 'Sufficiency thinking demands a transformation of human values, a 'revolution in the mind-set' necessary for the advances of human development' (UNDP, 2007, pxviii)

It is not possible here to do justice to all aspects of this Thai philosophy, policy and practice. In my judgement, the strategy of the Thai leadership is among the alternatives to what has been referred to as 'corporate globalization'. However, to be successful in gradually transforming human values in Thailand, new thinking is also needed internationally, for instance, concerning the WTO. A well-functioning democracy is probably another precondition for changes in ideological orientation and institutional arrangements.

Reconsidering institutions

Institutional change processes can be initiated by many actors and at many places in the economy. Institutional change may start, as we have argued, by reconsidering perspectives in a broad sense (theory of science, theoretical perspectives and ideological orientation) or in a more narrow sense (interpretation, naming and manifestation of specific phenomena). In both models the role of individuals as actors is essential. While there is path-dependence and pressure (in different directions) from other actors, there is also a potential for choice. In his book *When Corporations Rule the World*, David Korten refers to Willis Harman: 'By deliberately changing the internal image of reality, people can change the world' (Korten, 2001, p233).

Institutions may change through spontaneous action but also in more deliberate ways, such as new laws and other regulations. In the following discussion, I exemplify some areas where spontaneous change probably needs to be supplemented by new institutional arrangements.

Limited liability companies

The most common organization in our society is the joint stock company or limited liability company (this is referred to as a 'corporation' in the US). It has been argued that if SD is measured in multidimensional terms, we should not rely heavily on a kind of organization defined in one-dimensional monetary terms. Corporations accumulate resources of a monetary and non-monetary kind and have considerable power to influence contemporary society. If these organizations, according to law, have to focus only on their monetary responsibilities to shareholders, then they are also far from the ambition to extend ethical horizons, another imperative connected with SD. In short, these companies or corporations are not compatible with SD.

A number of business actors are aware of the tensions between normal business operations and societal objectives, such as those connected with SD. In this way we have seen the beginning of institutional change processes in the form of EMSs and an intensified debate about CSR, as previously discussed. This is far from enough. It is true that when the joint stock company was introduced it represented an institutional innovation that reduced risks and facilitated industrial production and trade and thereby contributed to a kind of material prosperity.[1] When describing our present market economy and capitalistic system, the joint stock company is at the centre. But society has changed partly because of the policies, lobbying activities and operations of giant business corporations. Today something new is needed if we seriously bother about SD and the survival of humankind.

Many small business companies that operate locally or regionally emphasize non-monetary objectives and do not necessarily maximize profits. Rather they look for satisfactory profits. Very high profits may indicate that a company is exploiting some stakeholder groups, such as suppliers, employees or customers. The big challenge is to find ways of transforming large corporations in a step-wise manner to middle-sized companies with mission statements of a multidimensional kind.

In this part, I have no final recommendations except for pointing once more to a conceptual framework in terms of institutional economics as previously described and a radical version of SD as the ideological orientation. Instead of relying exclusively on monetary accounting systems, non-monetary accounting systems have to be developed as part of a multidimensional and multiple-stakeholder perspective (Brown, 2000).

The World Trade Organization

International organizations, such as the World Bank and IMF have to leave their neoclassical and neo-liberal agenda behind. The task should no longer be one of facilitating life for trans-national corporations and their ideas about globalization (see for example Perkins, 2004). WTO and its sister organizations have played a leading role during a period when a large number of unsustainable trends have become visible. While one can consider reform, the possibility of dismantling these organizations should also be seriously considered. If policy recommendations and action based on one philosophy lead us in an unsustainable direction then further action based on the same or a similar philosophy will not be of much help. Civil society intellectuals together with different groups of professionals and citizens have long criticized the WTO for its narrow ideas about the impacts of trade. Employing additional persons who know of no other economics than the neoclassical kind will only aggravate the problems.

University departments of economics

Here the recommendations follow directly from previous chapters in this book. The naïve idea of value neutrality has to be abandoned. If each theoretical perspective is value-laden, then research and education at departments of economics have to become compatible with democracy. Rather than monopoly for neoclassical theory, competition and pluralism has to become the rule. Neoclassical economists need not be afraid of giving up everything, as in the case of a Kuhnian 'paradigm-shift'. A new 'equilibrium' will probably be established where some parts of neoclassical theory are judged appropriate for some purposes while other theories are more useful for other purposes. This is what has been referred to as 'paradigm coexistence'.

Economics is said – even in neoclassical textbooks – to be about 'choice'. Today students at departments of economics are denied the right to have an opinion on more fundamental issues, such as the choice among theoretical perspectives. Neoclassical economists will not easily give up their monopoly. They protect their interests, as can be predicted with reference to their own public choice theory (which is about 'rent-seeking' by specific interest groups). Only intervention from outside by politicians, by scholars from other disciplines, students, journalists or other actors may help. Here I will only make some comments on the so-called 'Nobel Prize in Economics'.

The Bank of Sweden Prize in Economic Sciences in Memory of Alfred Nobel

The ordinary Nobel prizes in physics, chemistry, medicine, literature and the Nobel Peace Prize carry with them a certain prestige. At the end of the 1960s, some leading neoclassical economists saw a chance of strengthening their position further by instituting a new prize in economics financed by the Bank of Sweden (Riksbanken). Since this time a prize in economics has been given to a number of economists who with few exceptions belong to the neoclassical camp. Gunnar Myrdal, regarding himself as an institutional economist, is one of the exceptions but when rewarded, the committee pointed to his early achievements in price theory before his questioning of the mainstream and declaring himself an institutionalist.[2]

While many are sceptical about the prize in economics, it certainly has a symbolic value to indicate 'the right kind of economics' and it is an instrument of power to protect the neoclassical paradigm. 'Economics' is then seen as equal to 'neoclassical economics' and those who do not accept this perspective are not economists or are confused persons. Those who want to be seen as candidates for the prize seldom use the term 'neoclassical economics' and even less question this paradigm. Even those who get the prize seldom refer explicitly to neoclassical economics. In a recent book *Making Globalization Work* by Joseph Stiglitz (2006), a respected economist and winner of the Bank of Sweden Prize, the term 'neoclassical economics' is not part of the subject index. The book has other qualities of a positive kind as will be commented upon later in this chapter.

What should one do about this prize? One option, and perhaps the most honest one, is to disconnect the prize from the name of Alfred Nobel and refer to a 'Bank of Sweden prize in neoclassical economics' or 'the Bank of Sweden memorial prize in neoclassical economics', since the award was instituted at the time of the 300-year anniversary of the Bank of Sweden. Another option is to abandon the idea of value neutrality by admitting that ideology is involved. In this case one has to articulate what is regarded as being in the interest of humanity and what is less exciting.

Abandoning the idea of value neutrality and accepting the coexistence of perspectives would mean a new beginning for economics and the prize. Since neoclassical economists lack competence outside their own paradigm, a new prize committee would have to be appointed. In my judgement, Swedish professors of economics were more broad-minded in the 1950s and 1960s than they are today. The prizes of the 1970s, the first decade that the prize was offered, went to persons who were reasonably open in relation to other disciplines and competing ideological orientations. Present professors of economics in Sweden are more narrowly oriented towards analysis and presentations in terms of mathematics and statistics.[3]

While the Bank of Sweden Prize remains a big problem, there exists another Stockholm-based foundation that can modify the picture of our responsibility in this country. This is an international institution, the Right Livelihood Award Foundation, which rewards persons and organizations 'for outstanding vision and work on behalf of our planet and its people'. As described on the home page of www.rightlivelihood.org, it:

> *celebrates and supports people of vision. People who have ideas and apply them to concrete situations. They give hope for tomorrow, for a world of peace and balance. They demonstrate how we can overcome oppression, war, poverty, the destruction of our environment, and a widespread sense of meaninglessness and fear.*

The awards of the Right Livelihood Award Foundation are sometimes referred to as 'alternative Nobel prizes'. The purpose of the Foundation is to:

> *promote scientific research, education, public understanding and practical activities which:*
> - *contribute to global ecological balance*
> - *are aimed at eliminating material and spiritual poverty*
> - *contribute to lasting peace and justice in the world.* (Right Livelihood Award Foundation, 2007, p10)

Since 1980, more than 125 individuals and organizations, many of them from developing countries, have received the Right Livelihood Award (RLA). Much like the Nobel Peace Prize, the RLA is based on relatively clear ideas about present problems and challenges and ways of dealing with them. Achievements in science are not excluded but have to be related to the purpose or value orientation of the Right Livelihood Award Foundation.

Reconsidering actor roles

Habits of thought and behaviour are parts of our PEP assumptions (see Figure 4.1). There are at the same time openings for new thinking and changes in behaviour. We can change our own thinking patterns and actions as well as our expectations of others. Even an individual's ideological orientation may change. Table 3.3 suggests that there is a choice with respect to worldview, including theory of science, disciplinary paradigm in economics and ideology.

The individual may be moving from a narrow to a broader idea of responsibility and accountability (see Table 3.4). The individual and his or her social, institutional and physical context change more or less over time. In a sense the social and institutional context of an actor at a point in time is given; in some other sense our actor chooses or selects other actors to cooperate with or relate to. An actor similarly faces some parts of the institutional context more than other parts and may have ideas and opinions about how to modify or change that institutional context.

The previous pages have focused on the role of economics in the present development dialogue. One of the messages has been that economists and other scholars cannot point to value neutrality and play innocent if things go wrong in society. We are all more or less responsible and accountable. Those who claim to know about the best steering or management philosophy, for instance by repeatedly pointing to 'optimal resource allocation', are not without responsibility for the unsustainable trends exemplified in this book.

Students of economics could follow the example of their French colleagues and articulate a demand for a pluralistic and less dogmatic economics.

Politicians could similarly follow the German example (see Chapter 1) and participate in a constructive debate about the future of economics. If economics departments and university professors do not understand that dictatorship in the sphere of paradigm (with connected ideology) is incompatible with democracy then power measures from outside have to be used.

While neoclassical economists claim to lead our societies towards increased welfare, some of us argue that problems are getting worse and that welfare, even survival, is threatened. A power game is going on at different levels from the role of science in society through theoretical perspective and ideological orientation towards institutional arrangements and practical measures. Whether unsustainable trends will prevail and be further strengthened or replaced by more sustainable ones is an open issue. As actors, we are all to some extent responsible and can use our voices to 'vote' for a sustainable society. But the premises or starting positions for participation in this power game may differ.

Action from below: Oscar Oliviera and Feng Xingzhongs

Listening to the stories told by individuals as actors is a way of learning about the problems faced in contemporary society. Some actors write their stories from an establishment position; they belong to a ruling elite. Others have to build their power positions from below and are dependent upon support from other actors who dare to challenge the ruling elite.

The stories that follow are all presented in books and are in that sense available. The purpose here is only to indicate the structure of the stories told and relate them to the kind of perspectives that have been articulated previously.

Questioning privatization of water in Bolivia

This case is presented in a book by Oscar Oliviera (2004) *Cochabamba! Water War in Bolivia*. At the time, Bolivia was under pressure from the IMF and the World Bank because of its external financial debt. The national government was weak and neo-liberalism was the dominant ideological orientation of establishment actors. The right to exploit natural resources, such as oil, gas and minerals were already largely in the hands of non-Bolivian corporations when the World Bank, in June 1999, issued a report on Bolivia to discuss the water situation in Cochabamba (Oliviera, 2004, p8). Privatization was a condition for loans and the Bolivian national government followed the World Bank recommendations and adapted the country's laws and regulations for this purpose. Later in 1999, a project to privatize water supply in Cochabamba was announced. Acquas del Tunary (Tunary Waters) received a 40-year contract to run the water system. Behind Tunary Waters was Bechtel and some other companies. Bechtel is a US company that is internationally active in infrastructure investments and operations.

Oscar Oliviera and many others felt that this was too much: 'Water is a fundamental human right and a public trust to be guarded by all levels of government, therefore, it should not be commodified, privatized or traded for commercial purposes' was among the arguments in 'the Cochabamba Declaration'. Oliviera worked from the position as labour union leader. However, many individuals from different segments of the Bolivian society joined him in a peaceful protest movement that ended with a cancelling of the mentioned contract. The archbishop of Bolivia played an important role towards the end of this conflict.

For the protest movement, neo-liberalism was the main enemy among ideologies. Neoclassical economics is not directly mentioned in Oliviera's book but obviously played a role in legitimizing neo-liberalism. Reference to 'commodification' can be connected with the neoclassical worldview. Among actors, the Bolivian government, the World Bank and the IMF were criticized for emphasizing the interests of business while downplaying the interests of the people living in Cochabamba.

Who is paying for our cheap imports from China?

In Sweden and other countries cheap jewellery can be imported from China and sold profitably. For Hammarby Sjöstad, a new development area for housing purposes, paving stones and other granite products have been imported in large scale (in spite of the abundance of granite in Sweden). Jewellery and granite products rely on factories for cutting stone, though people employed in these workshops may have problems with the work environment and lung diseases such as tuberculosis and silicosis. In their book *Sjukt billigt. Vem betalar priset för ditt extrapris?* (Suspiciously Cheap. Who is Paying for your Cheap Imports?), three journalists, Jörgen Huitfeldt, Thella Johnson and Ola Wong (2007) tried to uncover some of the challenges with Chinese exports and Swedish imports. Is it just a matter of low wages or is there something more? In their book, the authors give parallel stories about meetings in Sweden with those who market Chinese products, such as jewellery, those who present Chinese products at exhibitions in Hong Kong or elsewhere and actors connected with factories and production processes in the Chinese mainland.

Readers of this book can also learn about the fight for justice and compensation of one factory worker, Feng Xingzhongs, who suffers from lung diseases and was dismissed from his job when he could no longer work as before. He appealed for compensation but the factory owner and other establishment actors denied it. At some stage two organizations in Hong Kong, Labour Action China (LAC) and China Labour Bulletin (CLB) learned about his situation and supported him in his appeal. In the end, he received monetary compensation that was high when compared with similar cases in China but the compensation does not change the fact that he has to live with his occupational injury.

The conventional answer when asked about cheap imports from countries like China is to point to differences in wages. But the case presented also tells us about the environmental impacts in China of Swedish imports. This case clearly demonstrates the insufficiency of neoclassical trade theory (and neoclassical economics more generally) that focuses almost exclusively on the price of a commodity. It is easy to respond to this criticism by arguing that there are externalities and there is a PPP. However, in practice, payments for such externalities are seldom made (and if they are made, financial compensation will not change irreversible non-monetary processes). And externalities are not exceptions. They are abundant, and suggest that the price signals of the economic system too often are seriously wrong. As mentioned before, considering all externalities would bring us into a planned economy, something that market fundamentalists abhor.

Chinese workers suffer in terms of health (noise, vibrations, pollution) and are those who in a non-monetary sense 'pay' for the cheap imports to Sweden. But these workers are employed in the producer companies, which suggests a case of negative 'internalities' (rather than externalities). The families of these migrant workers suffer as well. Externalities in the traditional sense can also be observed. As part of the stone-cutting process, a lot of water is used to reduce particles in the air. In this way the work environment is improved a bit, but water is being contaminated. The particles are of different kinds. In addition to silicon, there is chromium, lead and arsenic, for instance. In a specific part of China, Fuding, the polluted water has affected crab breeding of farmers downstream. The tradition of shellfish cultures had to be given up, a tradition of more than 600 years (Huitfeldt et al, 2007, pp217–224). These problems are not easy to handle for the environmental protection administration in China but also Swedish import companies have a role and responsibility. CSR has to be translated into practice. Arguing in terms of the lowest possible price for specific qualities of paving stones (as in neoclassical economics) is too simplistic. This suggests that neoclassical economists writing books in international economics and trade theory also have some responsibility.

Action from above: John Perkins and Joseph Stiglitz

A case of dropout from the establishment

In his book *Confessions of an Economic Hit Man*, John Perkins (2004) tells us about his life story, which is closely connected with US ambitions to dominate the world. The term 'economic hit man' is explained in the Preface of the book (pix) as follows:

> *Economic hit men (EHMs) are highly paid professionals who cheat countries around the globe of trillions of dollars. They funnel money from the World Bank, the U.S. Agency for International Development (USAID), and other foreign 'aid' organizations into the coffers of huge corporations and the pockets of a few wealthy families who control the planet's natural resources. Their tools include fraudulent financial reports, rigged elections, payoffs, extortion, sex, and murder. They play a game as old as empire, but one that has taken on new and terrifying dimensions during this time of globalization.*
>
> *I should know; I was an EHM.*

Perkins was one of those 'highly paid professionals' but at some stage in his career he decided to move out of his position as EHM. Perkins gradually came to the conclusion that in countries where he had been an actor, such as Indonesia, Panama, Saudi Arabia, Iran, Colombia and Ecuador, poverty was not reduced as promised. Rather the opposite was true. He questioned the simplistic 'idea that all economic growth benefits humankind and that the greater the growth, the more widespread the benefits' (2004, pxii). The idea 'is of course erroneous' he continues. 'We know that in many countries economic growth benefits only a small portion of the population and may in fact result in increasingly desperate circumstances for the majority. ... A global empire of corporations, banks and governments, collectively the "corporatocracy" use their financial and political muscle to ensure that our schools, businesses, and media' support their ideas. Perkins also questions the idea that the 'captains of industry who drive this system should enjoy a special status. ... When men and women are rewarded for greed, greed becomes a corrupting motivator. ... Their mansions, yachts, and private jets – are presented as models to inspire us all to consume, consume, consume. Every opportunity is taken to convince us that purchasing things is our civic duty' (Perkins, 2004, pxiii).

Perkins does not refer directly to neoclassical economics or neo-liberalism but the spirit of his book is close to a criticism of these perspectives. Neither is SD part of his vocabulary, but again, he is very much concerned about the exploitation of natural resources and the suffering of indigenous people. The Perkins case can be described as one of radical positional change. His observations and experience made him start a new career more in line with his ethical concerns and ideological orientation. The story told by him is extremely important for channelling globalization in a more sustainable direction.

Criticism from within the establishment

In his recent book *Making Globalization Work*, Joseph Stiglitz (2006) tells us about his background as Senior Vice President and chief economist in the World Bank from 1997 to 2000, and about his many relationships with politicians in different parts of the world and actors connected with other international institutions, such as the IMF and WTO. In his acknowledgements, he also points to his meetings with winners of the Bank of Sweden Prize in economics in Memory of Alfred Nobel, such as Milton Friedman, George Stigler and Gary Becker. He expresses 'his gratitude to all of them for their patience and tolerance' (pxxii) in listening to his arguments about the limits of the market economy. According to Stiglitz, these limits have become accentuated with globalization and it is not clear that globalization brings prosperity to all. Instead, he argues there are losers in both developing and developed countries (pp8–9).

Stiglitz points to the need for reform concerning business corporations. He is even critical about the international institutions that he has served. Stiglitz discusses 'fair trade' as being different from mechanistic ideas about markets and is generally concerned about the world in which he lives.

While there are many openings for new thinking and a willingness to listen to many voices, for instance at the World Social Forum, Stiglitz is still the child of a period when neoclassical economics was the only paradigm taught in university departments of economics. He wants to modernize neoclassical economics, it appears, rather than look for other paradigms. While being critical of university education in economics as too slowly adapting to new realities, Stiglitz does not look outside mainstream literature. Fairness in economic affairs, for example labour relations, was discussed at an early stage by institutionalists, such as John R. Commons. When discussing schools of thought, reference is made to the tension between state and market and little else (Stiglitz, 2006, pp26–27). The terms 'neoclassical economics', 'paradigm' and 'pluralism' are not part of the subject index. But Joseph Stiglitz is still one of the most important economists today and, as I see it, 'moving in the right direction'. Being an establishment actor, there is a wide audience prepared to listen to his voice.

Epilogue

The debate about economics will continue. One of the first points raised in this book was that neoclassical economists and other economists have to abandon the idea of 'value neutrality'. Instead, one has to realize that values and ideology are always present in one form or other. Joseph Stiglitz reminds us that 'incentives matter' (2006, pxviii) and he does not exclusively refer to market or monetary incentives but also to possibilities of supporting or punishing people in other ways. There are market as well as non-market incentives and the choice between a policy based upon either type of incentive or a combination of both is a matter of ideology. In this work I have also pointed to the important role of what can be referred to as 'internal incentives', i.e. incentives from inside the individual as actor. This is covered by our concept of 'ideological orientation'. A given set of incentives from outside the individual, i.e. external incentives, may produce different behaviour depending upon the ideological orientation of the individual.

If we admit that we are in part guided by an ideological orientation even in the choice of perspectives, such as the economics paradigm referred to, many of the conflicts and tensions between mainstream and heterodox economists will be easier to understand and handle. In a democratic society, we do not need to agree completely about values and ideology. Some differences are instead thought of as being constructive for a debate about the future of society at the micro and macro levels. And such differences in ideological orientation may point in different directions with respect to relevant theoretical perspective.

A third point emphasized is that each individual as an actor matters. I have sympathies, for instance, with each one of the four persons presented in the previous sections. At different places and in different ways, they are working, at times even fighting, for what they see as a better society. From my point of view, from my scientific and ideological orientation, I feel there is much to do to get closer to a sustainable society. The market fundamentalism of neo-liberalism and much neoclassical economics is still important to deal with. However, there are also reasons for optimism.[4] The criticism expressed in academia and in larger social movements suggests that there are more options than one. All actors, as PEPs, have a role in participating in this debate and power game.[5]

Notes

1   See Micklethwait and Wooldridge (2003) for an account of the history of the joint stock or limited liability company where the adaptability to new circumstances is emphasized, and see Bakan (2004) for a sceptical view of such adaptive possibilities.

2   Myrdal only reluctantly accepted the award and expressed scepticism of this prize in economics more generally. He told me that he regarded it as an insult to share the prize with Friedrich von Hayek. Myrdal was a 'community-oriented' economist while Hayek was extremely market-oriented and is referred to as one of the fathers of neo-liberalism.

3   I have presented similar arguments in *Dagens Nyheter*, a leading Swedish newspaper but so far things remain essentially unchanged (Söderbaum, 2004d).

4   For those connected with universities, the proliferation of books about the role of universities in relation to the sustainability challenge is a reason for optimism (Hammond Creighton, 1998; Leal Filho, 2000; Barlett and Chase, 2004; Blaze Corcoran and Wals, 2004; Blewitt and Cullingford, 2004). But a lot remains to be done in universities, as elsewhere in society.

5   A final word about this book. As the reader has noticed, there are many references to Swedish experiences, even land-use planning in my home town, Uppsala, and also references to my own writings. This does not mean that the described Uppsala case is more interesting than other cases. The idea is rather that each person, wherever he or she lives, will find cases relevant from a sustainability point of view. Something similar holds for references to my previous writings. A lot of path-dependence is certainly involved but according to PEP assumptions, there is no reason to apologize for subjective experiences. Accepting pluralism means that there are always competing perspectives of a more or less subjective kind.

Further readings

Most participants in the development debate agree that globalization has to be given a human face. Something can be achieved through voluntary action but also new laws and other regulations, nationally and internationally, have to be considered. In her book *The Shock Doctrine. The Rise of Disaster Capitalism* (2007), Naomi Klein has pointed to how the present international economic system may invite some actors to behave in ways that many of us regard as cynical. Among establishment actors who exhibit signs of understanding that there is a moral aspect involved, Joseph Stiglitz and his book *Making Globalization Work* (2006) can once more be mentioned.

But many of us believe that also economics has to change and become more pluralistic. Edward Fullbrook's *Real World Economics. A Post-Autistic Economic Reader* (2007) is recommended for this purpose.

Questions for discussion

➤ One of the main institutions in our society is the company or corporation. The existence and performance of this kind of organization is defined in one-dimensional monetary terms. Do you think that it is realistic to expect companies to play a major role in the necessary transition toward an SD path?

➤ What is your opinion of the Bank of Sweden's Prize in Economic Sciences in Memory of Alfred Nobel? Is this an important issue at all, as you see it?

References

Ackerman, Frank and Lisa Heinzerling (2004) *Priceless. On Knowing the Price of Everything and the Value of Nothing*, The New Press, New York

Ashford, Nicholas A. (1981) 'Alternatives to cost-benefit analysis in regulatory decisions', *Annals of the New York Academy of Science*, vol 363, no 1, pp129–137

Attwater, Roger (1996) 'Participatory catchment management and economic method: An application in Thailand', *Asia Pacific Viewpoint*, vol 37, no 3, pp219–234

Bakan, Joel (2004) *The Corporation. The Pathological Pursuit of Profit and Power*, Free Press, New York

Barlett, Peggy F. and Geoffrey W. Chase (eds) (2004) *Sustainability on Campus. Stories and Strategies for Change*, The MIT Press, Cambridge MA

Barry, John (2007) *Environment and Social Theory* (second edition), Routledge, London

Berger, Peter L. and Thomas Luckmann (1966) *The Social Construction of Reality*, Anchor Books, London

Bebbington, Jan, Judy Brown and Bob Frame (2007a) 'Accounting technologies and sustainability assessment models', *Ecological Economics*, vol 61, pp224–236

Bebbington, Jan, Judy Brown, Bob Frame and Ian Thomson (2007b) 'Theorizing engagement: The potential of a critical dialogic approach', *Accounting, Auditing & Accountability Journal*, vol 20, no 3, pp356–381

Blaze Corcoran, Peter and Arjen E. J. Wals (eds) (2004) *Higher Education and the Challenge of Sustainability. Problematics, Promise, and Practice*, Kluwer, Dortrecht

Blewitt, John and Cedric Cullingford (eds) (2004) *The Sustainability Curriculum. The Challenge for Higher Education*, Earthscan, London

Bøgelund, Pia (2003) 'Greening the Area of Car Taxation? A Comparative Study of Environmental Policy Integration in Sweden and Denmark', Aalborg University, Department of Development and Planning, PhD thesis, Aalborg

Brown, Judy A. (2000) 'Competing ideologies in the accounting and industrial relations environment', *British Accounting Review*, vol 32, no 1, pp43–75

Brown, Judy and Bob Frame (2005) *Democratizing Accounting Technologies. The Potential of the Sustainability Assessment Model (SAM)*, Victoria University of Wellington, Centre for Accounting Governance and Accounting Research. School of Accounting and Commercial Law, Working paper series no 15, Wellington, New Zealand, www.victoria.ac.nz/sacl/CAGTRworkingpapers.aspx

Carson, Rachel (1962) *Silent Spring*, Penguin Books, Harmondsworth

Clark, Mary E. (1989) *Ariadne's Thread. The Search for New Modes of Thinking*, Macmillan, London

Clark, Mary E. (2002) *In Search of Human Nature*, Routledge, London

Clark, William C. and Nancy M. Dickson (2003) 'Science and technology for sustainable development, special feature. Sustainability science: The emerging research program', *Proceedings of the National Academy of Sciences of the United States of America* (PNAS), vol 100, no 14, pp8059–8061

Clayton, Anthony M. H. and Nicholas J. Radcliffe (1996) *Sustainability. A Systems Approach*, Earthscan, London

Commission of the European Communities (1998) 'Partnership for Integration. A Strategy for Integrating Environment into EU Policies. Cardiff – June 1998', Communication from the Commission to the European Council, COM(98) 333, CEC, Brussels

Commission of the European Communities (2001a) 'On the Sixth Environment Action Programme of the European Community "Environment 2010: Our future, Our choice"', CEC, Brussels

Commission of the European Communities (2001b) 'Consultation Paper for the Preparation of a European Union Strategy for Sustainable Development', Commission staff working paper, CEC, Brussels

Commoner, Barry (1971) *The Closing Circle. Nature, Man and Technology*, Alfred A. Knopf, New York

Connolly, William E. (1993) *The Terms of Political Discourse* (third edition), Blackwell, Oxford

Coote, Anna and Jo Lenaghan (1997) *Citizens' Juries. Theory and Practice*, Institute of Public Policy Research (IPPR), London

Cortright, S. A. and Michael J. Naughton (eds) (2002) *Rethinking the Purpose of Business. Interdisciplinary Essays from the Catholic Social Tradition*, University of Notre Dame Press, Notre Dame, Indiana

Dahl, Robert A. (1989) *Democracy and its Critics*, Yale University Press, New Haven

Dahl, Robert A. and Charles E. Lindblom (1953) *Politics, Economics and Welfare*, Harper & Row, New York

Dalal-Clayton, Barry and Barry Sadler (2005) *Strategic Environmental Assessment. A Sourcebook and Reference to International Experience*, Earthscan, London

Daly, Herman E. and John B. Cobb Jr (1989) *For the Common Good: Redirecting the Economy Toward Community, the Environment and a Sustainable Future*, Beacon Press, Boston

Dasgupta, Partha and Ismail Serageldin (eds) (2000) *Social Capital. A Multifaceted Perspective*, World Bank, Washington DC

Davis, Mike (2006) *Planet of Slums*, Verso, London

Dobson, Andrew (2004) 'Social inclusion, environmental sustainability and citizen education', pp115–129 in Barry, J., B. Baxter and R. Dunphy (eds) *Europe, Globalization and Sustainable Development*, Routledge, London

Dorfman, Joseph, C. E. Ayres, Neil W. Chamberlain, Simon Kuznets and R. A. Gordon (1964) *Institutional Economics. Veblen Commons, and Mitchell Reconsidered*, University of California Press, Berkeley

The Ecologist (1972) 'A blueprint for survival', *The Ecologist*, vol 2, no 1, January

Edlund, Jonas and Rodolfo Quintero (1995) 'Do Wabura – Farewell to the River! Application of Positional Analysis to the Urrá Hydro Power Plant in Columbia', Swedish University of Agricultural Sciences, Department of Economics, Report 94, Uppsala

Etzioni, Amitai (1988) *The Moral Dimension. Toward a New Economics*, Free Press, New York

European Council (2000) 'Presidency Conclusions', 23 and 24 March, European Council, Lisbon

European Council (2001) 'Presidency Conclusions', 15 and 16 June, European Council, Gothenburg

European Environment Agency (2005) *The European Environment. State and Outlook 2005*, European Environment Agency, Copenhagen

European Union (2001) 'Directive 2001/42/EC of the European Parliament and of the Council on the assessment of the effects of certain plans and programmes on the environment', 27 June, European Union, Luxenbourg

Faber, Malte, Thomas Petersen and Johan Schiller. (2002) 'Homo oeconomicus and homo politicus in ecological economics', *Ecological Economics*, vol 40, pp323–333

Fay, Brian (1996) *Contemporary Philosophy of Social Science*, Blackwell, Oxford

Ferber, Marianne and Julie Nelson (eds) (1993) *Beyond Economic Man. Feminist Theory and Economics*, University of Chicago Press, Chicago

Florini, Ann (2003) *The Coming Democracy. New Rules for Running a New World*, Island Press, Washington DC

Ford, David (ed) (1990) *Understanding Business Markets. Interaction, Relationships, Networks*, Academic Press, London

Forsberg, G. (1993) 'Finns ekologiskt hållbara energisystem? En uppföljning och konsekvensbeskrivninng för Kils kommun (Are there ecologically sustainable energy systems? The municipality of Kil as a case)', Swedish University of Agricultural Sciences, Department of Economics, Report 63, Uppsala

Frame, Bob and Judy Brown (2008) 'Developing post-normal technologies for sustainability', *Ecological Economics*, vol 65, no 2, pp225–241

Friedman, Milton and Rose Friedman (1980) *Free to Choose*, Penguin Books, Harmondsworth

Freeman, R. Edward (1984) *Strategic Management. A Stakeholder Approach*, Pitman, London

Fullbrook, Edward (ed) (2003) *The Crisis in Economics. The Post-Autistic Economics Movement: The First 600 days*, Routledge, London

Fullbrook Edward (ed) (2004) *A Guide to What's Wrong with Economics*, Anthem Press, London

Fullbrook, Edward (ed) (2007) *Real World Economics. A Post-Autistic Economics Reader*, Anthem Press, London

Funtowicz, Silvio and Jerome Ravetz (1991) 'A new scientific methodology for global environmental issues', pp137–152 in Costanza, R. (ed) *Ecological Economics. The Science and Management of Sustainability*, Columbia University Press, New York

Funtowicz, Silvio and Jerome Ravetz (1994) 'The worth of a songbird: Ecological economics as a post-normal science', *Ecological Economics*, vol 10, pp197–207

Funtowicz, Silvio, Jerome Ravetz and Martin O'Connor (1998) 'Challenges in the use of science for sustainable development', *International Journal of Sustainable Development*, vol 1, no 1, pp99–107

Fusfeld, Daniel R. (1994) *The Age of the Economist* (seventh edition), Harper Collins, New York

George, Susan (2000) 'A short history of neoliberalism: Twenty years of élite economics and emerging opportunities for structural change', pp27–35 in Bello, W., N. Bullard and K. Malhotra (eds) *Global Finance. New Thinking on Regulating Speculative Capital Markets*, Zed Books, London

Gillespie, Alexander (2001) *The Illusion of Progress. Unsustainable Development in International Law and Policy*, Earthscan, London

Glasson, John, Riki Therivel and Andrew Chadwick (1994) *Introduction to Environmental Impact Assessment*, UCL Press, London

Hajer, Maartens A. (1995) *The Politics of Environmental Discourse. Ecological Modernization and the Policy Process*, Clarendon Press, London

Håkansson, Håkan (ed) (1982) *International Marketing and Purchasing of Industrial Goods. An Interaction Approach*, Wiley, New York

Håkansson, Håkan and Ivan Snehota (eds) (1995) *Developing Relationships in Business Networks*, Routledge, London

Hall, Ralph (2006) 'Understanding and Applying the Concept of Sustainable Development to Transportation Planning and Decision-Making in the US', Massachusetts Institute of Technology, Cambridge MA, PhD thesis, http://esd.mit.edu/students/esdphd/dissertations/hall_ralph.pdf.

Hammond Creighton, Sarah (1998) *Greening the Ivory Tower. Improving the Environmental Track Record of Universities, Colleges, and Other Institutions*, The MIT Press, Cambridge MA

Harremoës, Poul, David Gee, Malcolm MacGarvin, Andy Stirling, Jane Keys, Brian Wynne and Sofia Guedes Vaz (eds) (2002) *The Precautionary Principle in the 20th Century. Late Lessons from Early Warnings*, European Environment Agency/Earthscan, London

Held, David (2006) *Models of Democracy* (third edition), Polity Press, Cambridge

Holden, Barry (2000) *Global Democracy. Key Debates*, Routledge, London

Howarth, David (2000) *Discourse*, Open University Press, Buckingham

Huitfeldt, Jörgen, Thella Johnson and Ola Wong (2007) *Sjukt billigt. Vem betalar priset för ditt extrapris?* (Suspiciously cheap. Who is paying for our cheap imports?), Norstedts, Stockholm

Humphrys, John (2001) *The Great Food Gamble. What We are Doing to our Food and How it Affects our Health*, Hodder and Stoughton, London

International Forum on Globalization (2002) *Alternatives to Globalization. A Better World is Possible*, Report drafting committee: J. Cavanagh, Co-chair, J. Mander, Co-Chair, S. Anderson, D. Barker, M. Barlow, W. Bello, R. Broad, T. Clarke, E. Goldsmith, R. Hayes, C. Hines, A. Kimbrell, D. Korten, H. Norberg-Hodge, S. Larrain, S. Retallack, V. Shiva, V. Tauli-Corpuz and L. Wallach, Berret-Koehler, San Francisco

Jackson, Norman and Pippa Carter (2000) *Rethinking Organisational Behaviour*, Pearson Education/Prentice Hall, Harlow

Jakubowski, Peter (1999) *Demokratische Umweltpolitik. Eine institutionenökonomische Analyse umweltpolitischer Zielfindung*, Peter Lang, Frankfurt am Main

Jakubowski, Peter (2000) 'Political economic person contra homo oeconomicus. Mit PEP zu mehr Nachhaltigkeit', *List Forum für Wirtschafts- und Finanzpolitik*, Band 26 (2000), Heft 4, pp299–310

Johansen, Leif (1977) *Samfunnsökonomisk lönnsomhet. En dröfting av begrepets bakgrunn og inhold* (Profitability at the societal level in terms of CBA. A conceptual study), Industriökonomisk institutt, Rapport, vol 1, Tanum-Norli, Oslo

Kapp, K. William (1950) *The Social Costs of Private Enterprise*, Shocken Books, New York

Kates, Robert W., William C. Clark, Robert Corell, J. Michael Hall, Carlo C. Jaeger, Ian Lowe, James J. McCarthy, Hans Joachim Schellnhuber, Bert Bolin, Nancy Dickson, Sylvie Faucheux, Gilberto C. Gallopin, Arnulf Grübler, Brian Huntley, Jill Jager, Narpat S. Jodha, Roger E. Kasperson, Akin Mabogunje, Pamela Matson and Harold Mooney (2001) 'Sustainability science (Policy Forum: Environment and Development)', *Science*, vol 292, Issue 5517, pp641–643

Klein, Naomi (2007) *The Shock Doctrine. The Rise of Disaster Capitalism*, Knopf Canada, Toronto

Korten, David C. (2001) *When Corporations Rule the World* (second edition), Kumarian Press, Bloomfield, Connecticut

Kras, Eva (2007) *The Blockage. Rethinking Organizational Principles for the 21st Century*, American Library Press, Baltimore, MD

Kuhn, Thomas S. (1970) *The Structure of Scientific Revolutions* (second edition), University of Chicago Press, Chicago, IL

Lapka, Miroslav, J. Sanford Rikoon and Eva Cudlínova (2007) *Is Globalization Overpowering Democracy? The Challenge for Ecology, Economy and Culture*, Dokoran Publisher, Prague

Leal Filho, Walter (ed) (2000) *Sustainability and University Life*, Peter Lang, Frankfurt am Mein

Legget, Jeremy (1999) *The Carbon War. Global Warming and the End of the Oil Era*, Penguin, London

Leipert, Christian (1983) 'Alternativen Wirtschaftlicher Entwicklung. Problembereiche, Ziele und Strategien', pp103–107 in Simonis, U. E. (ed) *Ökonomie und Ökologie. Auswege aus einem Konflikt*, C. F. Müller, Karlsruhe

Lenschow, Andrea (ed) (2002) *Environmental Policy Integration. Greening Sectoral Policies in Europe*, Earthscan, London

Lewin, Leif (2007) *Democratic Accountability. Why Choice in Politics is Both Possible and Necessary*, Harvard University Press, Cambridge MA

Lindblom, Charles E. (1977) *Politics and Markets*, Basic Books, New York

Lohman, Larry (2006) *Carbon Trading. A Critical Conversation on Climate Change, Privatization and Power*, Development Dialogue no 48, September, Dag Hammarskjöld Centre, Uppsala, Sweden

Mafunda, Dugushilu and Ståle Navrud (1995) 'Positional analysis applied to water pollution problems in developing countries', pp427–437 in Dinar, A. and E. Tusak Loehman (eds) *Water Quantity/Quality Management and Conflict Resolution. Institutions, Processes, and Economic Analyses*, Praeger Publishers, Westport CT

Marinov, Hristo (1984) *Ecologization*, Higher Institute of Finance and Economics, Svishtov

Martinez-Alier, Juan (1999) 'The socio-ecological embeddedness of economic activity: The emergence of a transdiciplinary field', pp112–139 in Becker, E. and T. Jahn (eds) *Sustainability and the Social Sciences. A Cross-disciplinary Approach to Integrating Environmental Considerations into Theoretical Reorientation*, (UNESCO, Paris) Zed Books, London

Micklethwait, John and Adrian Wooldridge (2003) *The Company. A Short History of a Revolutionary Idea*, Weidenfeld & Nicolson, Orion Publishing, London

Mishan, Ezra J. (1967) *The Costs of Economic Growth*, Penguin Books, Harmondsworth

Mishan, Ezra J. (1971) *Cost-Benefit Analysis*, Allen & Unwin, London

Mishan, Ezra J. (1980) 'How valid are economic evaluations of allocative changes?', *Journal of Economic Issues*, vol 14, no 1, pp143–161

Morgan, G. (1986) *Images of Organization*, SAGE, London

Mueller, D. C. (1979) *Public Choice*, Cambridge University Press, Cambridge

Myrdal, Gunnar (1972) *Against the Stream. Critical Essays on Economics*, Random House, New York

Myrdal, Gunnar (1978) 'Institutional economics', *Journal of Economic Issues*, vol 12, no 4, pp771–783

Naturvårdsverket, Miljövårdsrådet (Swedish Environmental Protection Agency, Environmental Management Council) (2007) *Miljömålen – ett internationellt perspektiv. Miljömålsrådets uppföljning av Sveriges miljömål, de Facto 2007* (Sweden's environmental objectives – an international perspective. A follow-up study by the Environmental Management Council, de Facto 2007), www.naturvardsverket.se/Documents/publikationer/620-1259-2.pdf (accessed 13 November 2007)

Norgaard, Richard B. (1989) 'The case for methodological pluralism', *Ecological Economics*, vol 1, no 1, pp37–57

Norgaard, Richard B. (1994) *Development Betrayed. The End of Progress and a Coevolutionary Revisioning of the Future*, Routledge, London

North, Douglass C. (1990) *Institutions, Institutional Change and Economic Performance*, Cambridge University Press, Cambridge

North, Douglass C. (2005) *Understanding the Process of Economic Change*, Princeton University Press, Princeton

O'Connor, Martin (ed) (1994) *Is Capitalism Sustainable? Political Economy and the Politics of Ecology*, Guilford Press, New York

Oliviera, Oscar (with Tom Lewis) (2004) *Cochabamba! Water War in Bolivia*, South End Press, Cambridge MA

Olson, Mancur (1965) *The Logic of Collective Action. Public Goods and the Theory of Groups*, Harvard University Press, Cambridge MA

Olson, Mancur (1982) *The Rise and Decline of Nations. Economic Growth, Stagflation and Social Rigidities*, Yale University Press, New Haven CT

Ostrom, Elinor (1990) *Governing the Commons. The Evolution of Institutions for Collective Action*, Cambridge University Press, Cambridge

Ostrom, Elinor (2000) 'Social capital: A fad or fundamental concept?', pp172–214 in Dasgupta, Partha and Ismail Serageldin (eds) *Social Capital. A Multifaceted Perspective*, World Bank, Washington DC

Passet, René (2000) *L'illusion néo-liberale*, Fayard, Paris

Pearce, David W., Anil Markandya and Edward B. Barbier (1989) *Blueprint for a Green Economy*, Earthscan, London

Pearce, David W. and R. Kerry Turner (1990) *Economics of Natural Resources and the Environment*, Harvester Wheatsheaf, New York

Pearce, David W. and Edward B. Barbier (2000) *Blueprint for a Sustainable Economy*, Earthscan, London

Perkins, John (2004) *Confessions of an Economic Hit Man*, Berrett-Koehler, San Francisco

Perlas, Nicanor (2000) *Shaping Globalization. Civil Society, Cultural Power and Threefolding*, Center for Alternative Development Initiatives (CADI), Quezon City

Porter Abbot, H. (2002) *The Cambridge Introduction to Narrative*, Cambridge University Press, Cambridge

Prugh, Thomas, Robert Costanza and Herman Daly (2000) *The Local Politics of Global Sustainability*, Island Press, Washington DC

Puskas Nordin, Anna-Carin and Peter Söderbaum (2004) 'Regionala aktörers tankar om hållbar utveckling. Kalmar och Uppsalaregionerna som exempel' (Thoughts about sustainable development by regional actors. The regions of Kalmar and Uppsala as cases), Mälardalen University, School of Business, Report 2004:1, Västerås

Ricoeur, Paul (1981) *Hermeneutics and the Human Sciences*, Cambridge University Press, Cambridge MA

Right Livelihood Award Foundation (2007) 'Illuminating the paths to a positive future', brochure, www.rightlivelihood.org, accessed 20 November 2007

Røpke, Inge (2004) 'The early history of modern ecological economics', *Ecological Economics*, vol 50, no 3–4, pp293–314

Røpke, Inge (2005) 'Trends in the development of ecological economics from the late 1980s to the early 2000s', *Ecological Economics*, vol 55, no 2, pp262–290

Roy, A. (2001) *Priset för att överleva* (The price for survival), Nya Doxa, Nora

Sachs, Ignacy (1976) 'Environment and styles of development', pp41–65 in Matthews, William H. (ed) *Outer Limits and Human Needs*, Dag Hammarskjöld Foundation, Uppsala

Sachs, Ignacy (1984) 'The strategies of eco-development', *Ceres. The FAO Review*, vol 17, no 4, pp17–21

Savitz, Andrew W. with Karl Weber (2006) *How Today's Best-Run Companies Are Achieving Economic, Social and Environmental Success – And How You Can Too*, John Wiley & Sons, Hoboken, NJ

Schumpeter, Joseph (1942) *Capitalism, Socialism and Democracy*, Harper & Row Publishers, New York

Self, Peter (1975) *Econocrats and the Policy Process. The Politics and Philosophy of Cost-Benefit Analysis*, Macmillan, London

Self, Peter (1993) *Government by the Market? The Politics of Public Choice*, Macmillan, London

Self, Peter (2000) *Rolling Back the Market. Economic Dogma and Political Choice*, St Martin's Press, New York

Sen, Amartya (1987) *On Ethics and Economics*, Basil Blackwell, Oxford

Shi, T. (2002a) 'Ecological economics in China: Origins, dilemmas and prospects', *Ecological Economics*, vol 41, no 1, pp5–20

Shi, T. (2002b) 'Ecological agriculture in China: Bridging the gap between rhetoric and practice of sustainability', *Ecological Economics*, vol 42, no 3, pp359–368

Shiva, Vandana (2002) *Water Wars. Privatization, Pollution, and Profit*, Pluto Press, London

Shiva, Vandana (2005) *Earth Democracy. Justice, Sustainability and Peace*, Zed Books, London

Simon, Herbert (1947) *Administrative Behaviour*, Macmillan, New York

Simpson, L. and K. Ringskog (1997) *Water Markets in the Americas*, World Bank, Washington DC

Söderbaum, Peter (1967) 'Profitability of Investments and Changes in Stock of Technical Knowledge', (mimeographed) licentiate thesis, Department of Business Studies, Uppsala University, Uppsala

Söderbaum, Peter (1973) *Positionsanalys vid beslutsfattande och planering. Ekonomisk analys på tvärvetenskaplig grund* (Positional Analysis for Decision-making and Planning. An interdisciplinary Approach to Economic Analysis), PhD thesis, Department of Business Studies, Uppsala University, Esselte Studium/Scandinavian University Books, Stockhholm

Söderbaum, Peter (1980) 'Towards a reconciliation of economics and ecology', *European Review of Agricultural Economics*, vol 7, no 1, pp55–77

Söderbaum, Peter (1982a) 'Ecological imperatives for public policy', *Ceres. FAO Review for Agriculture and Development*, vol 15, no 2, pp28–30

Söderbaum, Peter (1982b) 'Positional analysis and public decision making', *Journal of Economic Issues*, vol 16, no 2, pp391–400

Söderbaum, Peter (1991) 'Environmental and agricultural issues: What is the alternative to public choice?', pp24–42 in Dasgupta, P. (ed) *Issues in Contemporary Economics, Volume 3. Policy and Development*, International Economic Association, Macmillan, London

Söderbaum, Peter (1999) 'Values, ideology and politics in ecological economics', *Ecological Economics*, vol 28, pp161–170

Söderbaum, Peter (2000) *Ecological Economics. A Political Economics Approach to Environment and Development*, Earthscan, London

Söderbaum, Peter (2001) 'Political economic person, ideological orientation and institutional change. On competition between schemes of interpretation in economics', *Journal of Interdisciplinary Economics*, vol 12, no 3, pp179–197

Söderbaum, Peter (2004a) 'Democracy, markets and sustainable development: The European Union as example', *European Environment*, vol 14, no 6, pp342–355

Söderbaum, Peter (2004b) 'Politics and ideology in ecological economics', International Society for Ecological Economics, Internet Encyclopaedia of Ecological Economics, www.ecoeco.org/education_encyclopedia.php

Söderbaum, Peter (2004c) 'Decision processes and decision-making in relation to sustainable development and democracy: Where do we stand?', *Journal of Interdisciplinary Economics*, vol 14, no 1, pp41–60

Söderbaum, Peter (2004d) 'Nobelpriset i ekonomi – hinder för nytänkande', *Dagens Nyheter*, DN Debatt, 10 October, translated and republished as 'The Nobel Prize in Economics – A barrier to new thinking' pp81–83 in Fullbrook, E. (ed) (2007) *Real World Economics. A Post-Autistic Economics Reader*, Anthem Press, London

Söderbaum, Peter (2005) 'Actors, problem perceptions, strategies for sustainable development. Water policy in relation to paradigms, ideologies and institutions', pp81–111 in Biswas, Asit K. and C. Tortajada (eds) *Appraising Sustainable Development. Water Management and Environmental Challenges*, Oxford India Paperbacks, Oxford University Press, New Delhi

Söderbaum, Peter (2006) 'Democracy and sustainable development: What is the alternative to cost-benefit analysis?', *Integrated Environmental Assessment and Management*, vol 2, no 2, pp182–190

Söderbaum, Peter (2007a) 'Issues of paradigm, ideology and democracy in sustainability assessment', *Ecological Economics*, vol 60, pp613–626

Söderbaum, Peter (2007b) 'Paradigms, democracy and globalization: The role of actors, language and ideology in institutional change', pp34–61 in Lapka, M., J. Sanford Rikoon and E. Cudlínova (eds) *Is Globalization Overpowering Democracy?*, Dokoran Press, Prague

Söderbaum, Peter (2007c) 'Interpretations of sustainable development and corporate social responsibility in relation to paradigm and ideology: An actor-oriented perspective', pp232–255 in Ketola, T. (ed) *Paradigms of Corporate Sustainability*, Proceedings of Track 16, International Sustainable Development Research Conference 2007, University of Vaasa, Report 146, Vaasa

Stiglitz, Joseph (2006) *Making Globalization Work*, Penguin Books, London

Sunstein, Cass R. (2002) *Risk and Reason. Safety, Law and the Environment*, Cambridge University Press, Cambridge

Svenskt Näringsliv (Confederation of Swedish Enterprise) (2002) *Från defensiva till proaktiva. Företag och hållbar tillväxt* (A pro-active rather than defensive strategy. Business and sustainable development) (by Eva Bingel, Claes Sjöberg and Charlotte Sjöquist), Svenskt Näringsliv, Stockholm

Swedish Government (2004/2005) 'Sweden's environmental quality objectives', government web page summarizing Government Bill 2004/05:150, Environmental Quality Objectives: A Shared Responsibility, www.sweden.gov.se/sb/d/5775

Task Force Environment and the Internal Market (1990) *'1992' The Environmental Dimension. Task Force Report on the Environment and the Inner Market*, Economica Verlag, Bonn

Toulmin, Stephen (1990) *Cosmopolis. The Hidden Agenda of Modernity*, The University of Chicago Press, Chicago

United Nations (2007) *The Millennium Development Goals Report*, UN, New York, www.un.org/millenniumgoals/

UNDP (United Nations Development Programme) (2007) *Thailand Human Development Report 2007*, http://hdr.undp.org/en/reports/nationalreports/asiathepacific/thailand/name,3418,en.html

UNEP (United Nations Environment Programme) (2007) *Global Environmental Outlook GEO 4. Environment for Development*, www.unep.org/geo/geo4/media

Uppsala kommun (1997) 'Uppsala Agenda 21. Utgångspunkter för en god miljö och en hållbar utveckling' (Uppsala Agenda 21. Points of Departure for a Good Environment and Sustainable Development), Antaget av kommunfullmäktige (accepted by City Council) 27 October, Uppsala

Uppsala kommun (2005a) 'Förslag till översiktsplan för Uppsala kommun' (Proposal for Comprehensive Plan, Uppsala municipality), Kommunledningskontoret, Uppsala

Uppsala kommun (2005b) 'Strategisk miljöbedömning av förslag till översiktsplan för Uppsala kommun' (Strategic Impact Assessment of Proposal for Master Plan, Uppsala municipality), Tyréns, Stockholm

Uppsala kommun (2005c) 'Klimatstrategi för Uppsala kommun' (Climate Strategy for Uppsala Municipality), Antagen av kommunstyrelsen (accepted by City Council)16 October, Uppsala

Uppsala kommun (2006) 'Miljöprogram 2006–2009' (Environmental Management Programme 2006–2009), Antagen av Uppsala kommunfullmäktige (accepted by the local government) 27 March, Uppsala

Vogel, David (2005) *The Market for Virtue. The Potential and Limits of Corporate Social Responsibility*, Brookings Institution Press, Washington DC

WCD (World Commission on Dams) (2000) *Dams and Development. A New Framework for Decision-Making*, Earthscan, London

WCED (World Commission on Environment and Development) (1987) *Our Common Future*, Oxford University Press, Oxford

Williamson, John (1990) 'What Washington means by policy reform', in Williamson, John (ed) *Latin American Adjustment. How Much Has Happened?*, Institute of International Economics, Washington, DC

Williamson, John (2000) 'What should the World Bank think about the Washington Consensus?', *The World Bank Research Observer*, vol 15, no 2, pp251–264

Woodin, Michael and Caroline Lucas (2004) *Green Alternatives to Globalisation. A Manifesto*, Pluto Press, London

Zadek, Simon (2001) *The Civil Corporation. The New Economy of Corporate Citizenship*, Earthscan, London

Index